The Return
The Mulberry Tree

Two Plays about Palestine

Hanna Eady and Edward Mast

Fomite
Burlington, VT

For permission for professional or amateur production, public readings or any other performance of these plays contact:

The MARTON AGENCY, Inc.

1 UNION SQUARE WEST, SUITE 815

NEW YORK, NY 10003-3303

(212) 255-1908

info@martonagency.com

Both *The Return* and *The Mulberry Tree* are available in Hebrew translation. Contact the authors through the The Marton Agency.

ISBN-13: 978-1-959984-14-6
Library of Congress Control Number: 2023943136

Fomite
58 Peru Street
Burlington, VT 05401
www.fomitepress.com
10-07-2023

For the Eidi/Eady family spread around the world,

in the hope someday of return.

Contents

The Return

A Play in Four Scenes

THE RETURN premiered in 2014 at Al-Midan Theater in Haifa in a Hebrew translation by Oded Peled, directed by Sinai Peter. The English language premiere took place in 2017 at Mosaic Theater in Washington DC, directed by John Vreeke. The play has also been directed by Guy Ben Aharon at Israeli Stage Company in Boston in 2019, and directed by John Vreeke for Dunya Productions in Seattle in 2023.

CHARACTERS

HER

HIM

SETTING

The small front office of an auto repair garage in Herzliya, a mid-sized city in Israel.

Suggestion of a narrow counter with a tall stool behind it, and a padded bench for a couple of customers to sit. One entrance/exit behind the desk, another to the street for customers.

She wears street clothes. He wears auto-shop uniform.

Neither Arabic nor Israeli accents are called for in the play. The play was written in English but the imagined language that both characters speak in Israel would be Hebrew, and both characters are equally fluent.

The character Him is Palestinian, but nothing in his look, dress, or speech identifies him as non-Jewish. The story of the play is founded on the fact that, like many Palestinians who live inside Israel, the character Him can easily pass as Israeli Jewish.

None of this is to disqualify actors who happen to have those particular regional accents, but rather to note that we all have regional and international accents and in this case those should not be emphasized.

SCENE ONE

(They stand looking at each other.

Silence.)

                    HIM

Shalom.

                    HER

Shalom.

                    (Silence.)

                    HER

You're open.

                    HIM

We are.

                    (Silence.)

                    HER

I was surprised.
That you're open.
It's pretty late.

                    HIM

Yeah. Everybody's gone, but I can work on Shabbat. So we can get a little more done.

                    HER

Right. You can work on Shabbat.

                    HIM

I can.
Because I'm not, you know.

                    HER

One of us.

HIM

Right.

(pause)

Sometimes people can't tell.

(pause)

Don't want any confusion.

(pause)

I'm the only one here though, so.
We might not finish everything today.

(pause)

That your car?

HER

That? Yeah.

HIM

What's the uh
What can we help you with?

HER

Uh. Your sign says you only uh . . .

HIM

Yeah. We mostly deal with army jeeps, but we can take a look at it.

HER

That's what I was wondering. They let you work on army jeeps here?

HIM

Yes. We have a contract.

HER

Oh.

HIM

The shop. Not just me.

5

HER

Uh huh.

HIM

Yeah.

If you wanna come back when someone else is here, that's fine.

HER

No. No. I didn't mean that.

HIM

It's okay. I would understand.

HER

No no, this is fine.

HIM

Okay.

So.

What would you like us to look at?

HER

Uh.

Have you . . .

Have you worked here a while?

HIM

Why would you like to know that, Ma'am?

HER

Just curious.

HIM

No secret.

About seven, seven and a half years now.

HER

Good job?

                          HIM
It's fine. Are you an Inspector?

                          HER
                        (laughs)
No no no . . .

                          HIM
I can show you my work permit.

                          HER
No I promise, sorry, sorry. I'm just being nosy.

                          HIM
Okay. Well this is a fine place to work.

                          HER
Good.

                          HIM
I'm a little busy right now, everyone else is gone . . .

                          HER
And they let you work on those military vehicles.

                          HIM
Yes.

                          HER
Alone. By yourself.

                          HIM
Yes.
I have a permit. And a training certificate. If you're concerned.

                          HER
Any kind of special test for you?

HIM

Ma'am, I'm the only one here the rest of today. If you want to bring your car back when we're open again on Sunday, there'll be other guys here to look at it. Regular guys. No hard feelings.

HER

No that's not what I mean —

HIM

Or we can leave it with instructions, it'll be safe in the garage . . .

HER

No no please, I'm sure you're just as capable and trustworthy, there's no issue, I don't mean that at all.

HIM

Okay.

HER

In fact I wouldn't be surprised if you're more capable than some of them.

HIM

Lotta good mechanics here.

HER

Yeah?

HIM

Uh-huh.

HER

Do you get credit for all the work you do?

HIM

Sorry? What do you mean?

HER

I just wonder if sometimes you. Don't get credit for what you do?

HIM

Why would that be, Ma'am?

HER

Do you get paid the same as the others?

(Pause.)

HIM

They trust me fine here, Ma'am. And I'm paid just fine as well. You know, I really think you might wanna come back another day.

HER

No no.

HIM

I'm busy anyway, I wouldn't get to your car today . . .

HER

Listen . . .

HIM

We got lots of other guys, you can leave it for them if you don't wanna make another trip, I won't touch it.

HER

No no no no . . .

HIM

Sunday everybody's back.

HER

No that's not what I want. This is the time I want to be here. It's exactly the right time, as it turns out. But sorry. I just. I'm sorry. I just know that. Some people don't get treated fairly. That's all.

HIM

Huh.

HER

So I wonder what it's like for someone like you to work in a place like this.
I'm surprised to see you, I was surprised when you came walking out.
I'm surprised they let you work on those army vehicles by yourself. That's
great, I'm glad they do. But I just went through that security maze at the
airport. I've been away. I've been out of the country. For a while now.

(Pause.)

HIM

Have you.

(Pause.)

HER

Yeah. Quite a while. And I come back, a lot's changed. Do you have
the new cameras and scanners here?

HIM

Not yet. It's an old shop.

HER

And they let you work on army jeeps. Maybe that's good. But it's not
so good here. For some people. I'm not the only one who knows.
There are a lot of us who understand.

HIM

Understand what, Ma'am?

HER

You say they pay you fine.

HIM

Yes.

HER

They pay you the same as the others?

HIM

I don't know what they pay the others. Not my business.

HER

They pay you enough to support a family?

HIM

I don't know what it takes to support a family. They pay me fine.

(Pause. She sits on the bench.)

HER

I don't know either.

HIM

Don't know what?

HER

What it takes.
To support a family.

(Silence.)

HER

May I ask.
What your name is?

HIM

Yes Ma'am. My name is Yakov.

HER

Yakov.

HIM

Yes.

HER

Huh. That's an odd name for you to have.

HIM

It's pretty common.

HER

Is that your real name?

HIM

It's what they call me here.

HER

I see. Is that the name they gave you?

HIM

Ma'am, my name here is Yakov and you're welcome to use it. I have some work I'd really like to get done today if I can.

HER

Did they always call you that? Yakov?

HIM

Yes Ma'am.

HER

They never called you Avi?

(Pause.)

HIM

Ma'am, is there something wrong with your car that we can help with?

HER

No.

HIM

Then I'm gonna have to ask you to let me get back to my work.

HER

Not just yet.

HIM

Okay. We're done.

HER

No.
We're not.

HIM

(moves calmly to a spot behind desk)

Ma'am I have the same police alarm button as everyone else.

HER

A police button.

HIM

If you have something in mind, the officers will be here in no time.

HER

Have you ever used it?

HIM

No. Never had to.

HER

If you push that button, do you think they'll protect you? Against me? I don't know but I think they might not. It's terrible but it's true. I think they might not.

(She waits.)

HER

Avi.

(She waits.)

HER

What happened to the tattoo?

HIM

What tattoo?

HER

On your arm.

HIM

Ma'am. I don't know what you're looking for, but I don't think it's here.

HER

I know I look different. You do. It's been thirteen years and you have some new name. I don't know if that's real or a joke. Did they make you take a different name?

HIM

It's my name. You can examine my card and read the chip if you have a scanner, which I think maybe you do. I'm ready to cooperate as I always am. I don't think I've hidden anything, I'm sorry if I was supposed to respond in a certain way but I don't know anything about this new procedure you're doing . . .

HER

It's not a procedure.

HIM

Then what is this about?

HER

I'm sorry, I started all wrong. I didn't expect you to come walking out like that. And if you did, I expected you to tell me to get out the minute you saw me.

HIM

Why would I do that?

HER

Avi.

HIM

That's not my name.

HER

Are you playing a game, or do you really not recognize me?

HIM

Am I supposed to recognize you? Have you been in before?

HER

Here? No. Finding this place was a research project.

HIM

Why would you want to do that?

HER

Avi. Did anything happen to you thirteen years ago? Would you look at me closely please?

HIM

If you'll tell me what this is about, I'll do what I have to do.

HER

It's you. You're not that hard to find. We can access the records about you people, you know that.

HIM

Yes I know that.

HER

Will you tell me who you are?

HIM

I have told you.

HER

Please don't be scared.

HIM

What am I not supposed to be scared of, Ma'am?

HER

My name is Talia. Will you look at my face? If this is some kind of game, will you stop it? And if you really don't remember, will you look hard, and take thirteen years away from this face and this body I guess, and say hello to me for who I am?

(Pause.)

HIM

Thirteen years is a long time.

Lotta things happened back then, and before then and since then. What happened then isn't necessarily part of who I am now. If I'm supposed to remember something that I don't, I apologize. I'm sorry if it was important to you and I've forgotten. I know you checked the records and it's true that they keep careful track of people like me, but maybe you've still got the wrong person. There's other people who look like me. And other people who look like you. I'm sorry for your trouble, Ma'am, and I'm sorry to disappoint but I'm not whoever you're looking for.

(Pause.)

HER

Maybe not. And maybe you are, and this is hard for you in a way I don't understand. I believe my eyes and my ears and everything about you, but I can't make you admit something you refuse. Fine then. If you are not Avi, whose real name was Samer,

[pronounced "SAMMer" with rolled r]

then I apologize for upsetting you and taking your time, and I hope you'll forgive my mistake because the records point here and you look and sound exactly like him. Except he had a little tattoo on his arm and you don't.

HIM

It's okay Ma'am . . .

HER
(standing)

If you are Avi. Samer. You should know that I only came here. From very far away. Because. I think I may have done something wrong. To you. Something terribly terribly wrong. That's why I came back to look for you. I don't want any more trouble. I may have done something terrible to you, and if I did, then, I don't know. I'd like to make it right. I'd like to understand at least. That's all I want.

Now.

Avi.

Will you admit that it's you?

(Pause.)

(Pause.)

(Pause.)

HIM

Lady.

(Pause.)

HIM

I don't know what you're talking about.

(Blackout.)

SCENE TWO

HIM

Shalom.

HER

Shalom.

(Silence.)

HER

You're open.

HIM

We are.

(Pause.)

HER

It's late.

HIM

I can work on Shabbat.

HER

Right. You work on Shabbat.

HIM

Mmhmm.

HER

So everybody else is gone.

HIM

Yeah.

(Pause.)

HER

Lucky they have you.
To get that extra work done.
On those army jeeps.

HIM

I suppose so.

(Pause.)
(Pause.)
(Pause.)

HER

We've met.

(Pause.)

HIM

Yeah.

(Pause.)

HIM

You were in last week.

(Pause.)

HIM

You thought I was somebody else.

(Pause.)

HIM

I'm sorry I disappointed you. Did you ever find him?

(Pause.)

HER

Yeah. As a matter of fact.
I did.

(Pause.)

19

                            HIM

Good.

That's all cleared up then.

                          (Pause.)

                            HER

Some things.

                          (pause)

So you don't have the new cameras here?

                            HIM

Not yet.

                            HER

Are you sure?

                            HIM

They haven't installed them yet.

                            HER

At least not while you were here. You can't always see them, you know.

                            HIM

That's true. They're putting them everywhere though. I don't think they'll go to special trouble to hide them just for us.

                            HER

No?

                            HIM

Don't think.

                            HER

No special surveillance on this place?

HIM

Not that I know about.

HER

With all those army jeeps?

HIM

Just the usual. They have to be careful.

HER

I suppose. I'm not sure I'd call it just "careful" anymore.

HIM

They do what they have to do. Not up to us to figure out.

HER

No?

HIM

They have to keep us safe.

HER

Oh yeah? You feel safe now?

HIM

I guess.

HER

Hm.
I don't.
I don't feel safe.
Now that you mention it.
I don't feel safe at all.
I feel less and less safe. Every day.

HIM

You do look a little nervous.

HER

(laughs)

Nervous. That's funny. Nervous.

How about you?

You don't feel nervous?

HIM

Ma'am, has something gone wrong with your car?

HER

Not especially.

HIM

Did you come back to tell me you found that guy you were looking for?

HER

Sort of.

HIM

Well good. I'm glad. Thanks for taking the trouble.

HER

No problem.

HIM

So.

(pause)

So we're done.

HER

Yeah.

HIM

Okay then. I'll just uh. Have a good day.

HER

It's just that . . .
I dunno, I've been out of the country. Maybe I just don't uh.
I guess I'd like to ask your opinion.

HIM

About what?

HER

Something happened. And I wonder if it's normal, or even common
these days.

HIM

Does it have to do with me or this shop, Ma'am?

HER

Well here's the thing.
Last week. Last Friday, in the afternoon. When I was here. You
remember.

HIM

Mmhm.

HER

Right after I left. Right after you told me you were definitely positively
not the man I was looking for. You remember that.

HIM

Mmhm.

HER

I got stopped. Siren, the whole thing, they pulled me over.

HIM

For what?

HER

That's what I wondered. But you know how they talk, they don't tell you
anything, license please, where ya headed, they're curious I've been out

of Israel, in the U.S., you know. I'm bewildered, what, have they started arresting people for speeding? So I don't know what they want.

> HIM

Ma'am —

> HER

And they ask me where I've just come from.
And that puzzles me.
And I say Officers what's the problem?
And they say Just answer the question Ma'am. And I say Have I done something wrong? And they say Just answer the question Ma'am. And I say If you'll tell me what's going on, I'll be happy to answer and they say Answer the question, all polite like that, and I can't figure how it makes any difference to them, so I ask Am I under arrest? And they say Get out of the car Ma'am.

> *(pause)*

And they take me to a station that turns out to be not far away.
And they ask me more questions.
And it turns out they know where I've been.
They knew I had just come from here.

> HIM

How did they know that?

> HER

I don't know how they knew that. I still don't know how they knew. But they knew I had been here and they had a really good idea of who I was looking for.

> *(She waits.)*

> HER

They wondered why though. Some of them stayed polite, while others did not. The polite ones voiced concern. Why would I want to find this guy? What would I possibly want with him? Considering what he did to me?

(She waits.)

HER

They wondered if I was looking for some sort of trouble or payback
and they really wanted to discourage that sort of thing. I hadn't even
admitted I was here but I tried to assure them that I was not after that.
They knew how long I'd been out of the country. They knew when I
came back. They knew my whole story. And they knew all about the
guy I was looking for.

(She waits.)

HIM

Did they tell you where to find him?

HER

Yes.

(She waits.)

HER

I had plenty of time to think about everything they asked me. They
didn't pull out any surveillance video, they didn't say You came
and left at suchandsuch a minute. Plus I couldn't think of a single
reference they made to anything you and I talked about while I was
here. So I think you might be right. I think we're not being recorded. I
think there might not be any hidden cameras in here. Yet.

(She waits.)

HER

So I don't know. How they found out.
I can't think of a single person. Who knew. Or would tell them.

(She waits.)

HIM

I called them.

HER

Except you of course. Yeah.

(Pause.)

HER

Why?
Why did you call them?

HIM

I didn't think they'd bother you. I'm sorry for that.

HER

I don't understand. Do you work for them now?

HIM

I sure didn't think they'd pick you up. I don't know why they did that.
I'm sorry.

HER

Is that why they let you work on army jeeps?

HIM

No.

HER

Then I don't understand. Am I some danger? I don't understand.

HIM

No. You don't understand. You do not understand.

(He is beginning to be agitated)

HIM

I call them all the time. It's what I do.

HER

Are you alright?

HIM

I have to check in with them. On a regular basis.
If anything happens and they have to find out themselves, it can be a
problem.

HER

But nothing happened. I walked in the door and we talked.

HIM

Maybe it was nothing. It's not up to me to decide. If I don't report and they find out, it can become an irregularity. And there can be consequences.

HER

Like what?

HIM

I don't know. I always report. It's not up to me to decide what matters and what doesn't. That's up to them. I just check in.

HER

Are you on parole . . .

HIM

No.

HER

. . . or some kind of probation?

HIM

No. But there are conditions. For my special circumstance.

HER

What special circumstance?

HIM

What I did. The nature of what I did.

HER

What you were accused of doing.

HIM

What I did and was found guilty of doing in a court of law.

HER

Are you sure you're alright?

HIM

I'm fine, I will be fine when you are gone. Do you understand now? I had to call in and report. I had no idea what action they would take or not take, I'm sorry it was trouble for you, I don't want trouble for you, I don't want trouble for myself. I will have to call them again now. I'm sorry. But that is my special circumstance. That is my situation. Do you understand?

HER

You're on a list.

HIM

Yes I guess so.

HER

For ever?

HIM

As far as I know.

HER

Is there any way to get off it?

HIM

Not that I know of.

HER

Because of what I did.

HIM

No, because of what I did.

HER

I mean because I had you arrested.

HIM

You had every right to.

HER

And now you're on a list for all time, and your life is not your own.

HIM

It's not your fault.

HER

I think it is. I think it was always my fault. I think I committed a crime against you.

HIM

No you didn't.

HER

But I guess I thought it was over at least, you were back to some kind of normal. But you're not. It's forever.

HIM

I'm telling you it's not your fault. If I hadn't committed the crime I wouldn't be where I am now.

HER

You didn't commit a crime. I did. I knew it the minute I saw you again. I invented a crime out of nothing and I caused all this.

HIM

Ma'am I don't know what you want —

HER

Would you stop calling me Ma'am?

(pause)

You know what my name is. I'm the one who sat there calling you a criminal. I didn't know what I was doing. I was stupid and ignorant, I was surrounded by ignorance, I was surrounded by people telling me what I needed to do. I didn't understand. I came back here to try to understand, and now I think I do. I think I need to ask your forgiveness.

                                   HIM

You don't need to ask my forgiveness. I need to ask yours. I did
ask, back then. And I still do. I ask your forgiveness for the crime I
committed against you and against all of society.

                                   HER

Why are you saying that? There's no one else here. I'm not so young
and stupid anymore, we're standing here together and we both know
what really happened. You should never have been arrested.

                                   HIM

I'm glad I was.

                                   HER

Why?

                                   HIM

I'm glad they found me guilty, I'm glad for the sentence I got, I'm glad
for the time I spent inside. It gave me the space I needed.

                                   HER

For what?

                                   HIM

To understand where I went wrong and to turn myself around.
Learn auto mechanics. Come back into normal life and stop being a
criminal.

                                   HER

You were never a criminal. It's so clear now. You would never have
been arrested if you weren't what you are.

                                   HIM

A criminal.

                                   HER

No. An Arab.

HIM

Please stop.

HER

What? I didn't see it then, how could I, I was stupid like everyone else. But now it's so clear, I wonder how anyone can be so blind. I would never have turned around and brought the police into it, they would never have arrested you, you would never have been found guilty if you weren't a Palestinian Arab.

HIM

Stop.

HER

What's the matter with you? You think they would have arrested a Jewish guy?

HIM

If he was lying to you.

HER

What, if he told me he loved me but didn't mean it? If he told me he was single when he was married? Half the men in the country would be in jail. And you weren't even married. All you did was change your name to Avi to let me think you were Jewish. Do you know how many Israelis I met in the US who change their names to get laid? Yossi to Joe, Avram to Abe. But because you were Palestinian —

HIM

Stop it.

HER

What's wrong?

HIM
(gagging, bending down)

I'm begging you. Stop.

HER

What do you mean? It's the truth. You were only arrested because you were Palestinian —

HIM
(crumpling to the ground)
StooooOOOOOOOOOOOP!

(Blackout.)

SCENE THREE

(She sits alone.
He enters with paper cup of water.
Leans on desk.)

HIM

You're still here.

(She nods.
Pause. He sips his water.)

HIM

I thought you might be gone.

HER

You hoped.

HIM

Mm.

HER

Sorry.
I couldn't just walk away. I didn't know if you were sick.

(pause)

Are you sick?

(Pause.
He gives a little weary chuckle.
Pause.)

HER

Is there more of that?

(He goes.
Returns with another paper cup of water, rounds the desk and hands the cup to her. He moves away, finds a spot to sink to the floor and sit. They sip at their water.
Pause.)

                              HER

I guess I've ruined your work day.

                              HIM

Yeah.

                              HER

Will you get in trouble?

                              HIM

I don't know. You mean is there a work quota or something? No.
They're okay here.

                           (Pause.)

                              HER

What happened to the tattoo?

                              HIM

They had it removed.

                              HER

Why?

                              HIM

Didn't think it was appropriate for someone like me.

                              HER

Did it hurt?

                     (He shrugs a little.)

                              HER

You told me it was your grandmother's name, and she was from
Morocco. Remember? I had to find out in court. You weren't Jewish
from Morocco, and it wasn't your grandmother's name. It was the
name of the town where your grandmother lived. In what used to be
called Palestine. Isn't that right?

                           (Pause.)

34

HER

I wondered why anybody would do that. Tattoo the name of a town
on their arm. So I learned a little. What was the name? Is the town
gone now? One of those towns from 1948?

(Pause.)
(Pause.)

HIM

You said you've been out of the country.

(She nods.)

HIM

In the US you said. How long?

HER

Eight. Eight years.

HIM

Why'd you go?

HER

Wanted to get out of here.

HIM

Why?

HER

I don't know.
People changed.
When the trial was on, people said Oh you poor thing and How can
we help. And then the trial was over, but not the way people looked
at me. Or the way they didn't look at me. After a while a couple of
friends actually found ways to ask me What was it like? I couldn't
believe it at first. These were the same friends that made me go to the
police in the first place. But now they wanted to know if there was
some special charge, something electric or mysterious because you
were . . . you know.
And then some things would happen and I would not be invited.

Or someone wouldn't return my call. And then some tiny little comments would drop. And again I couldn't believe it at first. But they came around to wondering, and probably asking each other behind my back: how could you? With one of them?
Got so I felt surrounded, like some kind of wall.
I went to visit some friends in the US, it felt like escaping. A job opened up as a project manager, I decided to stay.

(Pause.)

HIM

I'm sorry.

HER

For what?

HIM

You had to go. That was my fault too.

HER

It wasn't you.
It was them.
It took me a long time to figure it out.
But then I realized.
They all knew the truth.
They knew it was me as much as you.
But they still thought you should go to prison for it.
That's when I started to look at living someplace else.
I could have accused you of anything.
I could have had you killed.

HIM

Yes you could have.
I'm thankful you didn't.

HER

Fuck I wish you would stop saying that.

HIM

I'll sign a statement if you want.

HER

What?

HIM

If they thought you knew. I'll sign a statement it was just me lying.

HER

So I can have my friends back here? Is that what you mean?

HIM

If it would help.

HER

Do you even remember what happened between us?

HIM

It wasn't between us. And no I don't remember if I can help it.

HER

Did you hold me down? Did you grab me? Did you jump me?

HIM

You never accused me of any of that. That's not the point.

HER

What is?

HIM

I tricked you.

HER

How? By saying I like to make love under the stars?

HIM

I lied.

HER

You didn't even lie.

HIM

I let you think it. So much for Arab pride. I was willing to give it all up just for that. I was willing to use any kind of trick, and pull out the darkened bedouin desert charm and you think ooh here's a nice Jewish boy with a little savage about him. But all that was true was the savage.

HER

Is that what they make you say about yourself?

HIM

It's the truth. I can try to deny it and resist it and make more trouble for everyone, or I can face it and try to live with it and manage it and have some peace and calm.

HER

God what they've done to you.

HIM

What I did to myself. What I am. What I did to you.

HER

It wasn't like that.

(He is shaking his head.)

HER

Did it happen just once?
Do you think I went off like that with just anyone?
Do you really not remember?

HIM

You must have believed my lying for that amount of time.

HER

You told them in court that I began it. That I, you know.

38

HIM

Please don't.

HER

I was the one who came back to the cafe. Without my friends.

HIM

You thought I was Jewish.

HER

Yes.

HIM

So I got your consent by lying. You thought you were having sex with Avi, not Samer. The court had to protect the public from sweet-talking sophisticated criminals like me.

HER

Yes I remember that phrase: sweet-talking sophisticated criminals. You're not a criminal. You had sex with a Jewish woman. That's why they sent you to prison.

HIM

Would you have gone with me if you knew I was Arab?

HER

No.

HIM

There then.

HER

I'm just trying to be honest. That's how I was then. That's not me anymore. I did something I regret and I want to make it better.

HIM

You are not making it better. You still don't understand. You put me in danger by walking in the door.

HER

I'm not dangerous! I want to help. It makes me sick, this place where someone goes to prison just because he's Palestinian.

HIM

Please can you go away. You've said. I've heard you. You don't understand.

HER

What?

HIM

I will have to call them again.

HER

Why? Nobody knows I'm here.

HIM

Maybe not, maybe so, some passer by through the window, some hidden something, some mistake, I don't know. If I don't tell them and they find out, it's all over.

HER

We're not doing anything, we're just talking.

HIM

Just talking.

HER

Yes.

HIM

That word. You said.

HER

What? What word?

(Pause.)

HER

Palestinian?

> *(He tries to resist the slight but definite physical effect the word has on him.)*

HIM

Yes.

HER

What's wrong with that? Have they made it illegal to say it now?

HIM

No. Yes. No. It is for me. I don't know what's illegal, that's the point. There are new things illegal here every day. And more unwritten illegal for me. For people like me.

HER

For Palestinians, you mean.

HIM

All we want is peace.

HER

Peace like the Iron Dome?

HIM

Yes.

HER

Like the peace checkpoints and the peace Wall and the peace security cameras and the hidden peace microphones?

HIM

They keep us safe.

HER

You mean it keeps people like me safe from people like you.

HIM

It keeps us safe too. Even me.

HER

Even you?

HIM

As long as I have nothing to hide. If I cooperate. If I'm good. If I'm careful and stay away from trouble. And that word . . . .

HER

You're Palestinian. It's just a word.

HIM

It's not just a word! It's an attack! It's a way of thinking! It's a way of believing that this whole country, your whole country, is not real, is not true, not fair, never really here, just a figment, some passing mistake, it's a way of saying we'll be back, we'll always make trouble, you'll never have peace, never ever, as long as we say that word, even to ourselves. It means war. It means trouble. It means never content, always looking back to the past, some imagined better past, some truth, some made-up truth that means nothing but blood and struggle and dying for nothing, that word means fear and war and torture, that word means everything I have to SQUASH if I'm gonna live through the day, I have to SMASH it, the war and the fight, if I smash them, if I eradicate them, if I work hard, every day of my life. And do my job. And live my life. One minute at a time. Then maybe. Maybe. I can have some peace.

I did my time, I paid my debt for what I did, I learned, I struggle every day to abide by certain conditions. Me and many others. We just try to stay quiet. Hold our heads down, even when things get bad, let them roll over us, stay quiet, maybe they won't notice us, maybe it will all stay normal. And then you walk through the door, like a missile. Like a bomb on somebody's belt. All I had to do was recognize you. And say out loud that you were you. For all that to come to an end.

Please. Will you leave before something worse happens. I can wait a while. Go to the airport, do what you have to do. I can wait. But I have to call them. I don't have a choice about that. I'm out here now on a thread. There are no second chances for people like me.

(pause)

All we want is peace.

(Pause.)

HER

There is no crime. Worse.
Than what they have done to you.
I don't know how they did this . . .

HIM

You don't want to know.

HER

And they burned off your tattoo. That was part of it. Right? They erased your family's town from your arm.

HIM

Didn't mean anything. I've never even been there. I was born in Haifa. It's somebody else's ancient history.

HER

Why did they care then? They want you to forget everything. And they want you to believe something happened between us that didn't happen.

HIM

It happened.

HER

Not like that. That's not how it was, that's not the truth.
The truth is.
It wasn't just the sex. Not for me anyway. I haven't come back for more, don't worry, I haven't been nursing some fantasy all this time. But the truth is we had a little something. Maybe it was just a fling,

but if it weren't for all this, this Peace Dome Security between us, we could have given it a chance. Maybe.

(Pause.)

HER

Can you say anything at all. Before you call them and turn us both in, whatever. Can you be just a person with me for a minute. And give me an honest answer? Was that all it was for you, was a trick? Or a quick one? Or a quick several? Can you say a word to me about how it felt for you?

(Pause.)

HIM

It felt real.

HER

Yes that's right. Me too. It felt real.
You knew I wasn't an Arab.

HIM

Didn't matter. You were just you. I guess I would have done anything. If I told you I was Arab you would have run away.

HER

Maybe.

HIM

So I guess I thought that I'd just be sincere and honest with my feelings. About you. And maybe by the time I told you the truth, you'd forgive me. Or the world would change.

HER

I wish you had told me and given me the chance. To be different.

HIM

You would have run away.

I guess so. But it broke my heart a little. You lying to me like that. When I found out, I wish I had gone to you and not to those friends that I thought were my friends. But it was too late. I didn't know what to think. Because you lied to me. And I let them talk me into it. Reporting you. Then everything happened by itself and I felt like I never saw you again.

(Pause.)

HIM

Maybe it could have been different.

HER

Maybe.

HIM

But here's another truth.

HER

About what?

HIM

You made me understand something. Back then.

HER

What?

HIM

That we could be together like that. You remember the way we kept our eyes open?

HER

Yes.

HIM

The way we touched our faces together? You remember that?

HER

Yes.

HIM

That we could be together like that.

HER

Yes we could.

HIM

And then.

HER

What?

HIM

And then you could be that other person. In the courtroom. Telling the story of what I did to you. Same eyes. Same face. Still you. But talking as if I was somebody else. Like you had the wrong person. And when I had time to think. Lots of time. I figured out that I wasn't just the wrong person. I was the wrong *kind* of person. I was born the wrong kind of person.

They helped me understand that in prison.

They were good at helping me understand that in prison.

About that town they took off my arm. About that word. And what I am.

That's what I have to remember. If I want any peace. Every day. Every minute. What I say, what I do, what I think. It's hard work. But I do it.

You made me understand that.

> (Pause.
> She moves over to him. Kneels on the ground, uncertainly. Bends down, touches her head to the ground before him.)

HIM

What are you doing?

> (She stays face down on the ground.)

HIM

Stop it. Please. Get up. What do you want? I accept your apology.
What do you want?

HER

(rising from her bow)

I want it to be better! I want it not to have happened! I want to be that
first person you knew. I want that other person in the courtroom to
never have existed. I want to go back to the way it was. I don't mean
us together now, it's the past, we're old, I'm old anyway. I don't mean
that. But I want us to just be people. Just people.

HIM

I'm sorry.

HER

What.

HIM

It's not as simple as that.

HER

Why not? What would it take?

HIM

Me to be somebody else. Or maybe not exist.

HER

That's not true. What if I go to them?

HIM

What do you mean?

HE R

You said you'd sign a paper. What if I go sign a paper? That I lied.
That I knew all along you were an Arab.

HIM

You'll go to jail. For lying in court.

                          HER

Maybe. Maybe that's what I deserve.

                          HIM

Don't do it.

                          HER

Why not?

                          HIM

I don't want you to go to jail.

                          HER

Even if it sets you free? After all this time? If they lift those
restrictions?

                          HIM

They won't believe you.

                          HER

They would have to!

                          HIM

Please don't.

                          HER

If you didn't have to call them ever again. If they didn't control what
you think. If you didn't have to tell them wherever you go. If you
could travel, wherever. Even out of the country and back. If you could
go anywhere. Where would you go?

                          HIM

I don't know.

                          HER

What about that town?

                          HIM

What town?

HER

The town they fucking burned off your arm. Your grandmother's town. Her village. I don't believe it didn't mean anything. I don't believe it. What if you could go there?

(No answer.)

HER

Samer. Some of us get it. We don't learn it in school but we can find out and I did. 1948. Four hundred of your towns destroyed. People driven out or killed and the towns buried. By us. Isn't that right?

(No answer.)

HER

If you could go there. Was it anywhere near here? Samer. I'd like to go there with you. I would like to go to your family's village. And stand there with you. Do other people live there now? Or is it just, I don't know what, ruins? Or some rocks? It can't be illegal to go stand there for a little while, is it? And if it is, I'll be there. They'll have to arrest me. Let them take me too.

(No answer.)

HER

This is what I want to do. With you.

(No answer.)

HER

Standing together on that village or whatever is there. Might make a difference. To me anyway. Maybe to you.

(No answer.)

HER

Is it close?

(No answer.)

HER

The site? The ruins or the location?

(No answer.)

HER

Do you know where it was?

(No answer.)

HER

Your village? Even if you don't, we can find it.

(No answer.)

HER

Samer. Do you know where your grandmother's town used to be?

(No answer.)

HER

They have no right to forbid you.
They have no right to forbid you!
They have no right to forbid you!
Samer. Do you know where your village was?

(No answer.)

(No answer.)

(He does not move.
Clenches eyes shut.
Turns face away.)

HIM

Up north.

(Neither of them moves.)

HER

In the Galilee.
What was its name?

HIM

Ein
Samara.

HER

Are you alright?

> *(Shakes head a little, eyes still clenched shut.*
> *She steps to him, slowly.*
> *Carefully reaches out, very lightly touches his hand. It*
> *does not startle him. He doesn't move.*
> *She takes a moment to choose the right words.)*

HER

Samer.
I will be there with you.

> *(Silence.*
> *Slowly he unclenches and opens his eyes.*
> *Turns his face.*
> *Looks at her.*

> *Blackout.)*

SCENE FOUR

(They stand looking at each other.)

HIM

Shalom.

HER

Shalom.

(Silence.)

HER

Are you still open?

HIM

We can close.

HER

Nobody else here, right?

HIM

Right.

HER

Okay.

HIM

Thanks for coming back.

HER

You said come back after work.

HIM

I wasn't sure you would.

HER

I said I would.

                         HIM

Yes I know. And you did.

                    (She nods.)

                         HIM

Listen. Talia.

                    (Pause.)

                         HER

What's wrong?

                         HIM

Nothing. Just, I've been thinking.

                         HER

About what?

                         HIM

Ein Samara.

                         HER

Your village.

                         HIM

Mmhmm. I've never been there.
They used to say there was a freshwater spring. And fig trees. There's
probably nothing there anymore. Just the place. Just dirt probably or
stuff they planted to replace it. I've thought about going there anyway.
Just to see the dirt, I guess. Or touch it. I couldn't of course, I can't,
they'll pick me right up. I'm not even supposed to say the name.
And then you're here. And I've said the name out loud. And it seems
possible. To go there and pretend there's a fig tree. And rub some dirt
between my hands. And just even stand there. Where it was. With
you.

                         HER

Yes.

HIM

I thought about running away with you. Someplace. Starting over.

HER

Me too. I thought about that too.

HIM

We're not so old.

HER

No we're not.

HIM

I would never have thought any of this. But you came back. You made me say that name. And I took back part of myself.

HER

I'm glad.

HIM

I have to tell you something.
I didn't call them.

HER

Of course not. I didn't think you would.

HIM

But I almost did.

HER

Why?

HIM

I need you to understand.

HER

I do.

HIM

You don't. You had a glimpse, you had a sample of what they do.

HER

So you have changed your mind.

HIM

I don't know. When you're standing here, you make it seem so possible.

HER

It should be.

HIM

But the minute you leave, it's different. There are things you can never know. No matter how much I try to tell you. I know it seems easy to you. But it's not.

HER

I know.

HIM

I've worked so hard. To be what they want me to be. I don't know how I can give that all up.

HER

So you think you might call them.

HIM

No. I will not betray you. What you have done for me now means too much.

HER

What?

HIM

I thought I would never trust a human again. Anywhere. I was positive. You've changed that. If you were an Arab and suggested that we go to the village site, I'd shut you up and kick you out. Ridiculous, dangerous, suicide. Especially for me. If they find out, I'm back in prison at least, and that's if I'm lucky. But for one of you. For one of you to be interested. Even interested. I didn't know it was possible. So I listened. And I want to believe. That there's hope.

> HER

I'd like to believe that too.

> HIM

I didn't know I could want such a thing, I didn't think I was able, but I was mistaken and you have made me understand that, and I thank you for it.
And I can't go with you.

> HER

Why not?

> HIM

We could not possibly keep it secret. There would be no chance. Maybe it's already too late, but this is just conversation. They would find us there.

> HER

How?

> HIM

Who knows how? Satellites, drones, I don't know. Even if it's not illegal for some, it's illegal for me. If they arrest us together, they take you one place, they take me someplace else.
I can't come. I want to. But I can't. I can't even walk through that door with you.

> HER

Why not?

> HIM

You might never believe it, you might never see it, because you might never know what it's like to be one of us and not one of you. It's not just me. Everybody like me, all the time. Big things, little things, need a permit, need approval, stop and hesitate, is it okay to do this, is it okay to own this, it never goes away. Will they pick me up, will I disappear. Every day, will I make it home tonight. It's hard for you to understand, because it's not the same for you. They've built this place where you and I can never be the same. As long as they keep running it this way, I can't walk through that door with you.

HER

So.

HIM

So this is our time then. Just this, right now. This is better than what we had or what we could have. This is our moment together. I'm glad you came back. I wish you could stay. I wish it could be different. I wish we could start over.

HER

Me too.

HIM

I'm sorry I can't show it to you. The color of the sky and the ground. I would love to show you. I'm sorry that it will never happen and that I'll never say these words again. But nothing will make me forget. Not ever. It doesn't matter whether I see it or stand there. It's something I have.

(hand on his chest)

I can't go with you there now, but it's something I have. And nothing they do to me can take that away. Ever. Ever. Ever.

(Pause.)

HER

Goodbye then, huh?

HIM

Yes. Goodbye. Thank you. I had given up but I have hope again. Thank you.

HER

Goodbye. *(lifts her arms uncertainly)* Can we . . .

HIM

Best not.

HER

Alright. Goodbye.

> *(Pause. They keep looking at each other.)*
> *(Pause.)*
> *(Pause.)*

HER

There's something you should know.

> *(Pause.)*

HER

I love you.
I have always loved you. Even when I didn't know it.
That's the part of me that I had to smash. And squash.
Because my world taught me
that loving you was a crime.
I love you, and I hope you know it.
And I hope you remember it.
No matter what happens.

HIM

I will.

> *(She nods a little.*
> *Pause.)*

HER

Is there a back door here?

HIM

What?

HER

A back door?

HIM

A back way out? You afraid someone will see you?

HER

You should use it.

HIM

What do you mean?

HER

I can distract them for a while. Go out the back way.

(Pause.)

HIM

How long have they been out there?

HER

They came with me.

HIM

You brought them.

HER

They would have come no matter what. I begged them to let me talk to you first.

(Pause.)

HIM

So everything you said was a lie.

HER

No. Everything I said was the truth.

(Pause.)

HER

I decided to go back to them. When you said come back after work, I had all afternoon, so I thought I could at least begin the process of telling the truth and filling out an affidavit to clear your record.

HIM

I told you not to.

HER

I know. I thought it would be a wonderful surprise. Even if they arrested me or something, as long as it cleared your name. I kept imagining how you would feel if I did that. It felt like the right thing to do. I was certain of it. I didn't tell them I came back here today, I didn't implicate you. I did everything so carefully.

HIM

And what happened?

HER

They said no thanks. Statute of limitations, no thanks. I said it would change his status, they started shouting, I shouted back, I said He's not dangerous, he just wants to live here like everyone else. And they said Leave it lady, he's fine, and I said He's NOT fine, there are places he can't even go! And they said Like where?

(pause)

And I shut up. But they said Where, lady? Has he been talking about his village again?
And I said No, but they said That's fine, Lady. Thanks for your help. We'll take it from here. We need to bring him in anyway. And I said No, you're wrong, what do you mean? but they wouldn't listen. They said You don't get it lady. It's not just him. What if they all went back to those villages? Do you know how many of them there are? What would happen? Would it still be Israel then? Do you care about Israel? Do you care about this country, Ma'am? Do you know what's there right now, in that place he calls his village? It's a city, it's Kiryat Avivim, it used to be nearby but the city got bigger and now what he

60

calls his village is under Kiryat Avivim. People live there. Where do you want those people to go? If you give it back to the Arabs, where do you want those people to go?

(Pause.)

                    HIM

So.
It's under Kiryat Avivim already.

                    HER

Yes.

                    HIM

We would have been too late anyway.

(Pause.)

                    HIM

So that's it then.

                    HER

No.
There's more.

                    HIM

What.

                    HER

Because for just one moment.
I thought:
they're right.
Kiryat Avivim. It's a city. I know people who live there.
So when they said Where you want those people to go,
I thought:
They're right.
There are too many.
Of you.

HIM

There's room for all of us here.

HER

I know. I knew it then.
But still, for a moment, I felt that other thing, for just long enough, I
felt it in my stomach, like a tumor, for one instant
I felt
that for this little place, this one little refuge in all the world
to be ours, you would have to . . . .

(She is unable to finish.
Finally:)

HIM

Not exist.

(Pause.)

HIM

So you understand now.

HER

Yes.
They couldn't just let you be.

HIM

They can't let any of us just be.
They would have found something. Sooner or later.

HER

Sooner or later.
I'm sorry it was me.
I thought I could save you by being good.
But everything I've done has been wrong.

(Pause.)

HIM
(does not look at her)

Do you want me to forgive you?

(Pause.)

HER

They said it will just be questioning.

HIM

Do you believe them?

HER

No.

(She looks outside.)

HER

They're waiting for you to go outside.

(Pause.)

HIM

Let them come in and drag me out.

I'm through taking orders.

(Pause.)

HER

If you tell me to leave, I'll go away.
If you tell me to stay, I'll stay with you.

(Pause.
He walks over near her, looks out the toward the street.)

HIM

Can they see us?

HER

Yes.

HIM

Good.

(He looks toward the street.
Looks at her.
Lifts an arm to reach out.

She steps to him.
They kiss, long and hard.
Police lights through the window on them.)

the end

The Mulberry Tree

A Play in Two Acts

THE MULBERRY TREE will premiere at La Mama Theater in New York in February 2024 in a production directed by Alexandra Aron for Loose Change Productions. An earlier version of the script has been translated into Hebrew by Leah Gilula and is available on request.

CAST OF CHARACTERS

Groupings indicate suggested doubling for a cast of six: 2 F, 4 M:

Noor	male, 10 to 38 years old
Zakariya	male, 60 years old
Grandpa	male, 60 years old
Kokab/Kokhava	female, 30 to 55 years old
Salma	female, 30-40 years old
Haya	female, 10 years old (voice)
Yitzhak	male, 35-45 years old
Uncle Tofeek	male, 30-40 years old

SETTING

Palestine which becomes Israel, 1942 -1970

ACT ONE

(The play opens in a small mountainside town in the Upper Galilee of what is now Israel, not far south of the Lebanese border. The year is 1970, three years after Israel conquered and occupied the West Bank, the Gaza Strip, and the Golan Heights. The town is almost exclusively Jewish, though it was not always so. The village retains many of the narrow streets and thick-walled limestone buildings from the past, mixed now with modern buildings which spread down the mountain and are spreading across the valley below.

None of this is represented on the stage itself. The play will take place in the imagination of the audience, and also the imagination of Noor, who is standing alone onstage. Noor is a 37-year old man who is well-dressed in a casual way. He is staring out past us without moving. He is silent for some time.

An older woman enters to one side behind Noor. Her name when Noor last saw her was Kokab. She wears a head scarf which does not cover all of her hair, and one of her everyday dresses: full-length, long-sleeved, flowing and colorful. By her clothing, we cannot tell if she is Jewish or Arab. She does not want to startle Noor, so she stops some distance behind him.)

KOKAB

Hello. Can I help you? I'm sorry, I was with a student group for a while.

(Silence. Noor does not turn to look at her.)

KOKAB

The museum is still open.
And the synagogue.
Or maybe you want to walk up to the cave?

(Silence. Kokab takes a step forward but not too close.)

KOKAB

You've been standing there for a while. Are you alright?

(Silence. He still does not turn or look at her.)

KOKAB

The museum is right this way.

(pause)

The cave is a little walk up the hill, but you probably have time before it gets dark.

(pause)

Or if you want to —

NOOR

That house.

KOKAB

Sorry?

NOOR

(points past us at an angle)

That house there. Is that part of your museum?

KOKAB

That? No. The museum's over here, if you want to —

NOOR

Who lives there now?
Do you know them?

KOKAB

Of course.

NOOR

Are they good people?

KOKAB
(*friendly smile, though wondering what's up*)
We're all good people here.

NOOR
They have a metal gate now. With a lock.

KOKAB
We like to keep safe.

NOOR
Safe.
Sure.
Those walls around the courtyard. They're higher.

KOKAB
Higher than what?

NOOR
You put up the stone wheel from the old olive press to decorate the village entrance. Nice idea. Just one wheel though. Where's the other one?

KOKAB
I guess you've been to our village before?

NOOR
(*still not turning to her; refers to a different spot past us*)
Those walls around your synagogue. They're higher too. The old mulberry tree still reaches over though. Is the old pomegranate tree still inside?

KOKAB
I'm sorry. Have we met?

NOOR
I'm taller now too.

(*He finally turns to face her. Silence.*)

> KOKAB

Noor.

> NOOR

Yes. Hello, Kokab.

> KOKAB
> *(slight pause)*

Kokab is not my name anymore.

> NOOR

I beg your pardon. Your Hebrew name then. How are you, Kokhava?

> KOKAB

I'm very well, thanks for asking. You must have come a long way to be here.

> NOOR

I live in Nablus.

> KOKAB

You got a permit to come from the West Bank?

> NOOR

Don't need a permit. The war's over. Everything's Israel now.

> KOKAB

I see. It's been twenty years then.

> NOOR

Twenty-two.

> KOKAB

Little Noor, all grown up. Well, Noor. Welcome to Israel.

> NOOR

Thanks.

> KOKAB

I hope you haven't come back looking for trouble.

NOOR

Trouble.
No.

                         KOKAB

I'm glad. What brings you then?

                         NOOR
                  (pauses, turns to look past us)
That house.

                         KOKAB

What about it?

                         NOOR

Maybe I'd like to buy it.

                         KOKAB

Buy it?

                         NOOR

Sure. What do you think?

                         KOKAB
                  (chuckles with disbelief)
You can't buy that house.

                         NOOR

What if they want to sell it?

                         KOKAB

They can't sell it to you.

                         NOOR

Why?
Because I'm not Jewish?

KOKAB
(evenly)
Because you're from a different time.

*(Silence. Noor looks toward another house off
past her.)*

NOOR
That was Abu Kamal's house. How long has it been a museum?

KOKAB
Long time now. The government set up a special fund for museums of
our local history.

NOOR
(nods)
I was in there. While you were with the students.
You have my grandfather's wooden plow on display.
And my grandmother's baking pan for thin bread.
Are we a part of this local history?

KOKAB
(pauses)
Not specifically.

NOOR
No? What do you tell people?

KOKAB
The topic doesn't come up.

NOOR
So you don't tell them anything.
Not even that we vanished? Or faded away?

KOKAB
We have plenty of our own history to tell.

(Silence.)

                    NOOR

You know, I read about this village.

                    KOKAB

Did you?

                    NOOR

Yeah. After Israel invaded the West Bank –

                    KOKAB

After Israel came home to the West Bank.

                    NOOR
              (takes a beat, continues)
We started to get Hebrew newspapers and some magazines. I
would pick one up sometimes, and once in a while there would be
something about this village. They call it by your new Hebrew name.

                    KOKAB

It's not new.

                    NOOR

And they talk about the cave, and the Zohar, and the old synagogue
with its ancient floor.

                    KOKAB

Do they? That's nice.

                    NOOR

And they would talk about the kindly old rabbi who kept the Jewish
traditions alive here before it was Israel. And how the old rabbi
welcomed the European Jews when they came. Here to this Jewish
village. This ancient Jewish village.

                   (Pause.)

                    NOOR

Did your father call it that? An ancient Jewish village? Or did they
just say that about him?

(Pause.)

KOKAB

My father didn't like newspapers.

(points to one side)

His grave is over there. Did you see it?

NOOR

I'll pay my respects.

KOKAB

You do that. And then why don't you be on your way.

NOOR

Where?

KOKAB

Back where you came from, Shkhem.

NOOR

It's Nablus.

What are you gonna do? Call the police?

KOKAB

Not right away.

NOOR

Come on, Kokab. It's just me.

KOKAB

That's not my name. And you could be anybody now.

NOOR

I see. Well. As the Zohar says.

KOKAB

What?

NOOR

"If I banish you, wolves and bears might kill you. But what can I do
with you?"

KOKAB

(takes a beat)

Well look at you. Quoting the Zohar after all these years. With your
outdated Hebrew that won't fool anyone. For old time's sake, I hope
you've had a nice look around. It'll be dark soon. I don't suggest
staying here after that. I hope you mean it, that you haven't come back
for trouble. We've never wanted trouble here.

*(She goes. He stares after; then turns to look toward
the grave she pointed out; then out toward us.)*

NOOR

Rabbi.
You remember me?
I wasn't going to come back.
But it hurt more to stay away.
I didn't know till I got here how bad it would feel.
To stand here.
In your Ancient Jewish Village.
Maybe you really didn't remember.
Or maybe you worked hard to forget. I can remind you.
You were the rabbi who wore a kufiyeh.
I was the boy who should have died but did not.

*(Behind Noor, enter Zakariya, an old man. He is
wearing a kufiyeh. He is looking and listening.
Noor does not turn around to see him.)*

*Zakariya is a Rabbi, but he wears a Jewish yarmulke under his
Arab kufiyah because in his time, Jewish Arabs and Arab Jews
were common and would both be considered Palestinian.
Zakariya wears European-style coat and trousers with
white shirt along with his yarmulke and kufiyeh.)*

ZAKARIYA

Someone there?

(Noor does not turn around to see him because he is in Noor's memory of the village in 1942. For the moment, Noor continues speaking out past us toward the gravesite.)

NOOR

The old mulberry tree was always taller than the wall between our houses.

ZAKARIYA

Is anybody there?

(Another actor as stagehand tosses on a cloth sack which lands on the ground with a crunch. Zakariya looks up as if at a tree.)

ZAKARIYA

What's that? Who's up there?

(At the dropping of the sack, Noor steps away to one side, turns to watch Zakariya, and now gives voice to an invisible boy in the invisible tree. Noor speaks in his normal voice, not a child's voice, although in character.)

NOOR

Nobody.

(In this scene, Noor would be 10 years old, but we do not see young Noor. Even though the adult Noor is standing at one side of the stage, we will watch this memory scene through Noor's eyes. He does not see himself, so we don't either. When Zakariya and other characters speak to the young Noor in this scene, they speak to an invisible boy. The adult Noor with his

*voice, and the other actors with the direction of their
eyes and attention, will help us imagine the young
Noor in the scene.*

*The adult Noor stays at the side of the stage, watching
the story unfold, giving voice to the young Noor, and
sometimes leading us through the story by reminding
the Rabbi what happened.*

*In the village as Noor remembers, neighbors would
commonly live so close together that their flat-roofed
homes would share one of the thick limestone walls, even
sometimes with a window in the wall. Some homes might
have a small fenced or walled courtyard in front, and those
side walls might also be shared with neighbors. As we will
learn, it happened that Noor's family shared a wall with
Zakariya's home, which was in the same walled compound
as the synagogue. Noor is remembering a mulberry
tree which grows in Zakariya's courtyard but spreads its
branches over the wall to the neighbors. The branches
spreading over the wall present an irresistible temptation to
the young Noor.)*

ZAKARIYA
(looks at invisible boy in tree branch)
Noor? What are you doing in the tree?

NOOR

Nothing.

ZAKARIYA

Shame on you. You come to steal mulberries?

NOOR

I didn't.

ZAKARIYA

From your uncle Zakariya? Why don't you just ask? Does your grandfather know you've been climbing up to steal berries?

NOOR

I didn't come up here to steal anything.

ZAKARIYA

What are you then, a silk worm weaving a sweater?

NOOR

Um –

ZAKARIYA

Well come down from there and leave our berries alone. Here, I'll catch you. Let go. Jump.

> (He helps the invisible boy come down. Behind them and from the same direction as Zakariya, a middle-aged man has wandered on and is watching: Yitzhak, who is dressed elegantly in light-colored European summer clothes.)

ZAKARIYA

Alright, I've got you, come on, there. Next time ask, say Uncle Zakariya I want some mulberries and I'll say Welcome, ahlan wasahlan.

NOOR

I wasn't –

YITZHAK

What's in the bag?

NOOR

Nothing — mamoul —

YITZHAK

Mamoul?

NOOR

I dropped it —

ZAKARIYA

Yitzhak, this is Noor, from right next door.

YITZHAK

Oh yes, Noor, Assad's boy.

ZAKARIYA

Noor likes to help himself to our mulberries sometimes.

NOOR

I hate berries.

ZAKARIYA

What?

NOOR

They give me diarrhea. I wasn't coming for that. I had to get here before sundown because I was coming to, you know.

YITZHAK

You were bringing mamoul?

NOOR

No. Yes I was but . . .

ZAKARIYA

Coming for what?

NOOR

To be your Shabbat helper.

ZAKARIYA

You were?

NOOR

Grandpa says you can't do things on the Shabbat, like light the fire, so some of us who aren't Jewish come help.

ZAKARIYA

Yes that's right. And they sent you this time?

NOOR

Yes.

ZAKARIYA

Is your grandpa sick?

NOOR

No. I asked if I could come do it.

ZAKARIYA

You did?

NOOR

Yeah.

ZAKARIYA

Why?

NOOR

Cuz.

ZAKARIYA

Hm. Well that was very gracious of you, little man. I'm honored. How old are you now?

NOOR

Ten.

ZAKARIYA

Well God bless you and I'm very grateful for your help. Look at this young friend, Yitzhak. Is this what you want to defend us from with your gifts?

YITZHAK

You and your jokes. So what's the bag for, kid?

(Zakariya picks up the bag.)

NOOR

Grandma made some mamoul. For your daughter to take to the
Jewish immigrants at the camp.

ZAKARIYA

Did she? That was very kind of her. Mamoul! Did you see that,
Yitzhak?

YITZHAK

Yes, I remember. Your grandma's the baker, isn't she?

NOOR

Yes.

YITZHAK

Well I can smell how delicious her baking is, Noor. You're a nice
neighbor. In fact you're such a nice neighbor, the Rabbi thinks that
solves everything in the world.

ZAKARIYA

Maybe not everything, but –

YITZHAK

He forgets that our people had nice neighbors back in Poland too.
Before that changed.

ZAKARIYA

The Nazis are not coming here. Didn't you hear the broadcast?
Rommel was defeated in Egypt.

YITZHAK

El Alamein, of course. Good news! But it's not just Nazis, Rabbi.

ZAKARIYA

Your toys from the British will not keep us safe.

YITZHAK

They're not toys –

ZAKARIYA

Any more than your special night squads kept us safe.

YITZHAK

Some people they did.

ZAKARIYA

Yitzhak, look around, will you? Do you see danger here?

YITZHAK

By the time you see it, it might be too late. Do you listen to the radio or do you only read your ancient books?

ZAKARIYA

The radio reaches my ancient ears, yes, and we are not Europe. You know us, Yitzhak. We've always been safe here together.

YITZHAK

So far.

ZAKARIYA

Always nice to see you. And thanks for the postcards. That's a nice photo of the village. They're popular in the shop so bring some more next time if you can.

YITZHAK

I will. And we can continue our conversation. You'll need more than a gate to keep safe. Nice to see you, Noor. Ten years old, you said?

NOOR

Yeah.

YITZHAK

Tell me something.

NOOR

What?

YITZHAK

You'd fight for your country, wouldn't you?

NOOR

Sure.

YITZHAK

There you go. *(to Zakariya)* Seems harmless now, huh? Just you wait. *(to invisible boy)* Tell your family that Yitzhak says hello.

NOOR

Okay.

> *(Yitzhak goes.)*

NOOR

Why did he ask me that? Is there a fight?

ZAKARIYA

Because he's thoughtless and no there is not a fight. Never mind him. You sure you don't want some berries while we're here?

NOOR

They make me ill.

ZAKARIYA

Oh that's right.

> *(Kokab calls from offstage.)*

KOKAB

Papa!

ZAKARIYA
(calling back)

Out here in the yard, Kokab.

> *(Enter Kokab. A grown woman, but twenty-eight years younger than opening scene.)*

KOKAB

Yitzhak just went past me and wouldn't hardly talk. What happened?

ZAKARIYA

He didn't get the answer he wanted.

KOKAB

Oh, Papa.

ZAKARIYA

We don't need what Yitzhak is offering. We're safe. We live together here.

KOKAB

I wish you'd read a newspaper.

ZAKARIYA

They're two weeks old by the time you get them.

KOKAB

Still newer than your Zohar. Some around here would be grateful for what Yitzhak is offering.

ZAKARIYA

Well maybe one of them should be rabbi. Yitzhak comes from Poland, he's one of these Europeans who bring their Europe ideas and don't understand how we live here.

NOOR

What is Yitzhak offering?

KOKAB

Noor? What are you doing here?

ZAKARIYA

Young Noor has come to —

KOKAB

Noor, it's late. Did your mother send over something?

ZAKARIYA

No, he was trying to steal some mulberries.

NOOR

I wasn't –

KOKAB

Noor, you know better than that. You steal our berries, I'll break your head.

ZAKARIYA

She really will.

KOKAB

You tell all your little friends too. I'll break their heads.

NOOR

I wasn't stealing berries!

KOKAB

You better not.

NOOR

My mom sent some mamoul.

KOKAB
(as Zakariya hands her the bag)
Mamoul! Why didn't you say so?

NOOR

For your people at the immigrant camp.

KOKAB

That's more like it. Papa, why are you spreading bad stories about him? Thank you very much, Noor, and thank your mother too. *(looking in the bag)* We've got fifty people at the camp and they love your grandma's mamoul . . . wait. What's this?

NOOR

Mamoul.

KOKAB

They're all broken.

ZAKARIYA

Oh, the bag dropped.

NOOR

Sorry. I was in a hurry to get here.

ZAKARIYA

Oh well, we don't want to welcome our immigrants with crumbs. We'll enjoy them here.

KOKAB

How, with a spoon?

NOOR

Sorry.

KOKAB

Don't worry, and tell your grandma thanks anyway. Take some berries home, if you like.

ZAKARIYA

They give him diarrhea.

KOKAB

Really? Then why was he trying to steal them?

NOOR

I wasn't –

KOKAB
(ruffles the invisible boy's hair)

Juuuust kidding. Don't make me break your head, though. You want to come in? I can't make you tea tonight but we might have some sweets.

ZAKARIYA

Noor has come to be our Shabbat helper.

KOKAB

Has he? What a good little man, thank you Noor. I'll put these away.
Papa, we can't keep sending Yitzhak off angry.

ZAKARIYA

He wasn't angry, just persistent.

KOKAB

He'd like to see something different from our rabbi.

ZAKARIYA

He's not part of my congregation.

KOKAB

What congregation? The one that came for Passover?

ZAKARIYA

The whole village came.

KOKAB

Exactly.

NOOR

I came. With Grandpa.

KOKAB

You were skipping pages during the ceremony.

ZAKARIYA

So I skipped the less interesting parts. That's why they call it Pass Over.

KOKAB

Oh Papa.

(going off after Yitzhak)
You tell your grandma thank you for these, Noor.

NOOR

Okay.
My Grandpa reads newspapers.

Abu Assad reads newspapers? Good for him. *(to Zakariya)* Maybe he won't be caught by surprise.

> *(She goes off.)*

NOOR

Is Kokab upset?

ZAKARIYA

(walks with invisible boy)

Oh, don't worry. Kokab works hard at the immigrant camp, and sometimes she gets annoyed at her old dad futsing around in his dusty synagogue.

> *(They walk around the empty stage, but their eyes and movements show that they are entering a special building with many very old books and relics and a floor of ancient tiles.)*

NOOR

How old is this synagogue?

ZAKARIYA

Oh very very old. The floor is about two thousand years old.

NOOR

Two thousand years?

ZAKARIYA

The walls not so much. That one about four hundred years. The rest we rebuilt not so long ago. Your father cut the stones.

NOOR

My dad did?

ZAKARIYA

Oh yes. He was a very good stonecutter. He was a good man. Your dad. I knew him when he was a boy. I miss him. Here, do me this favor and light the candle on that bookshelf.

                              NOOR

There?

                            ZAKARIYA

Yes, right in front of the Torah.

                              NOOR

I have a Torah, it doesn't look like this.

                            ZAKARIYA

This one is ancient. Don't touch! It's delicate. You have a Torah?

                              NOOR

Yes, I have two. The same one you gave to my grandpa, and he bought
me another one from the market, in Arabic

                            ZAKARIYA

Hm. What do you think?

                              NOOR

I like all the miracles. Moses and the Ten Commandments in Egypt.
Parting the water with his staff.

                            ZAKARIYA

So you read a lot?

                              NOOR

Well yeah. That's why I . . .

                            ZAKARIYA

Sorry?

                              NOOR

That's why I wanted to, you know. Come here.

              (Zakariya has been puttering about, listening but not
              giving close attention to the invisible boy. Now he
              turns and looks at the spot where the invisible boy is

standing.)

ZAKARIYA

Why?

NOOR

Because

(shyly steps toward the spot where Zakariya is looking)

Grandpa says you have lots of books.

ZAKARIYA

Ahhhh, I see. That's very true, I do. Though your Grandpa has books too.

(Gradually and without marking a major change, Noor has stepped into place as the boy. From this moment on, he is physically in the scene with Zakariya.)

NOOR

Yeah he brings me books from the market in Saffad every week. And Grandma reads her Russian books all the time.

ZAKARIYA

Yes, your communist grandmother. Ever since she learned Russian in school, her books are too thick for me.

NOOR

What's that one?

ZAKARIYA

That's the Zohar. Put another candle there.

NOOR

What's that?

ZAKARIYA

You have a good eye for books. The Zohar is very special. A very long time ago, a famous Rabbi escaped from the Romans. Rabbi Shimon

Bar Yokhai. He had to hide in a cave for thirteen years and during all those years he wrote the Zohar.

                    NOOR

Wow.

                    ZAKARIYA

He had to live on carob pods and water from a spring. Do you know what spring?

                    NOOR

No.

                    ZAKARIYA

Our spring here.

                    NOOR

Ours?

                    ZAKARIYA

The cave is up on our mountain. That's where Rabbi Shimon hid from the Romans and wrote the Zohar.

                    NOOR

Wow. What's it about?

                    ZAKARIYA

Ohhh, I don't think I would try to sum up the Zohar. It's in Hebrew of course. You don't read Hebrew?

                    NOOR

No.

                    ZAKARIYA

Well perhaps you'd be interested in this.

          (He reaches toward an invisible bookshelf, is handed a
          simply bound manuscript, which he holds out to Noor.)

NOOR

What is it?

ZAKARIYA

I've been translating some small bits of the Zohar into Arabic. You
might be able to read this passage here:

(He finds a page, opens to it, hands to Noor.

ZAKARIYA

This is the story of the Alphabet of Creation. "And each of the letters
of the alphabet entreated that the world be created through them."
Give it a try. If you like it, I can show you more.

NOOR

Wow. I know all the Hebrew letters.

ZAKARIYA

Well, maybe we can teach you a little Hebrew sometime. Would you
like that?

NOOR

Sure!

ZAKARIYA

We'll talk to my cousin Leah. She's good with that. But first in Arabic.

(opens the book and points to a page)
Look at this line here. Can you read it?

NOOR

(reads haltingly)
Open slightly your heart to me, and I will reveal to you the world.

ZAKARIYA

Good. Would you like to borrow this?

NOOR

Yes please.

GRANDPA
(from offstage)

Hello, hello.

ZAKARIYA

Hello! We're in here.

GRANDPA
(entering)
Good evening. How is our Shabbat helper doing?

ZAKARIYA

Splendidly so far. We'll see how good a fire he can make.

GRANDPA

Noor will do a good job. Won't you?

NOOR

Yes Grandpa.

GRANDPA
(handing a small bag to Zakariya)
Listen, I brought something for Kokab's immigrants at the camp.

ZAKARIYA

What is it?

GRANDPA

I saw them trying to make a garden. They don't know what they're doing. You can't just throw seeds in the ground. It's July. You need starters.

ZAKARIYA

Oh, right.

GRANDPA

So these are starters for tomato and red pepper.

                    ZAKARIYA
Excellent. Thank you.

                    GRANDPA
So. Is he gone?

                    NOOR
Who?

                    GRANDPA
Yitzhak.

                    ZAKARIYA
What, you didn't want to say hello?

                    GRANDPA
I wasn't in the mood. And?

                    ZAKARIYA
And what?

                    GRANDPA
Was he here for the usual?

                    ZAKARIYA
Yes.

                    GRANDPA
And you told him?

                    ZAKARIYA
The usual.

                    GRANDPA
I thought so. I heard him slam the door to his car.

                    NOOR
The usual what?

GRANDPA

Nothing.

ZAKARIYA

Nothing important.

GRANDPA

He's making headway though.

ZAKARIYA

How?

GRANDPA

Tofeek saw some of the Jewish settlers over at the kibbutz. The British were training them with Enfield rifles.

NOOR

Rifles?

(Grandpa and Zakariya stop, look at Noor standing between them.)

NOOR

Is that what Yitzhak wanted to bring here?

(Pause while they look at him. Then Grandpa decides.)

GRANDPA

Yes. Rifles and other weapons from the British.

NOOR

For us?

GRANDPA

No. For the Rabbi and his people. The British give them guns but not us.

NOOR

Why not?

GRANDPA

Because we mounted a revolt against the British. You remember.

NOOR

My dad.

GRANDPA

Yeah. The Rabbi's people had their own revolt against the British
but the British still give them weapons and not us. It doesn't matter
because our friend the Rabbi says no to Yitzhak whenever he brings
his nasty toys. There's your answer, now never mind and forget it.
Whatever Yitzhak wants, it won't happen here. Am I right?

ZAKARIYA

It won't happen here. Not while you and I are still around, huh?

GRANDPA

That's right. Let's help our Rabbi build his fire.

NOOR

I can do it.

GRANDPA

I know you can. I'll watch. And then we'll go home.

NOOR

Rabbi?

(*They stop.*)

ZAKARIYA

Yes Noor?

NOOR

Are you our Rabbi?

ZAKARIYA

Am I your Rabbi?

GRANDPA

What do you mean, "our"?

NOOR

I donno. You just called him Our Rabbi.

GRANDPA

I guess I did.

ZAKARIYA

Well I am the only rabbi in this village.

GRANDPA

So you must be our rabbi, Huh?

ZAKARIYA

I suppose so.

NOOR

Why don't we go to synagogue then?

ZAKARIYA

That is a very good question. *(to Grandpa)* Why don't you go to synagogue?

GRANDPA

Cuz we're not Jewish.

NOOR

Oh. What does that mean?

ZAKARIYA

It means you go to the mosque instead.

NOOR

We do?

ZAKARIYA

Yes. Don't you?

NOOR

When?

GRANDPA

When what?

NOOR

When do we ever go to the mosque?

GRANDPA

Sometimes. We went on Ramadan.

NOOR

Oh yeah. But people from the synagogue came then too.

ZAKARIYA

That's true. Even I went to the mosque during Ramadan.

GRANDPA

Of course they do. They come to the mosque to break the fast with us because they're friends.

NOOR

Oh.

GRANDPA

As much as we can be these days.

NOOR

What does that mean?

GRANDPA

Oh, the British make it tough to be friends sometimes.

NOOR

How?

GRANDPA

Never mind all these questions. We're friends, we go to the synagogue sometimes too. On special days. Like Passover.

NOOR

But we're not Jewish.

GRANDPA

No.

NOOR

What about the people who go to the church?

GRANDPA

Christians. What about them?

NOOR

Are we all friends?

GRANDPA

Sure, mostly.

NOOR

Cuz they believe in God too, right?

GRANDPA

Sure.

NOOR

Do we believe in God?

ZAKARIYA

That is another very good question, Noor. *(to Grandpa)* Do you believe in God?

GRANDPA

I don't know. Ask your grandmother.

ZAKARIYA

Oh we know what she'll say.

GRANDPA

That's true.

How do we know?

GRANDPA

Your grandmother is a communist. Even if she did believe in God, she'll never admit it. Tell you what: when we're in the mosque or the synagogue, or the church like on Easter, you go ahead and believe in God. Just in case your Grandmother is wrong.

NOOR

Okay.

GRANDPA
(as they start to walk off)

Let's see how you make that fire, then off for home, then maybe I'll come back for some backgammon later.

ZAKARIYA

Please do.

NOOR

But it's Shabbat.

(They look down at the invisible boy.)

NOOR

Playing backgammon. Isn't that work?

ZAKARIYA

Not when I play against him.

GRANDPA

Ohoho. Maybe you can move the pieces for the Rabbi and give him a chance of not losing so bad.

ZAKARIYA

God will grant victory to the righteous.

(Enter Salma, a woman in young middle age. She zeroes in on Noor.)

                    SALMA
Noor.

                    NOOR
Yeah?

                    SALMA
Did you go near Yitzhak's car?

                    NOOR
When?

                    SALMA
Today.

                    NOOR
No.

                    SALMA
Are you sure?

                    NOOR
Yes, Mom. I've been here.

                    GRANDPA
What's wrong?

                    SALMA
Someone punctured one of his tires.

                    GRANDPA
On his fancy car?

                    ZAKARIYA
Uh-oh.

                    NOOR
I didn't do it.

SALMA

He's hopping mad. He'd come yell but he doesn't want to step away from the car.

(Enter Kokab. To Salma:)

KOKAB

What does he say?

SALMA

He says it wasn't him.

KOKAB
(to Noor)

Is that right, Noor?

NOOR

I didn't do it!

KOKAB

Who then?

NOOR

I don't know! I was with Mom then I came here with the mamoul. I didn't even go outside, I used the tree.

KOKAB

Okay. I believe you. Your little friends though. This isn't like stealing mulberries.

NOOR

I wasn't –

KOKAB

I know I know. (to Salma and others) What do we do about Yitzhak? He's bothering Abu Hanna about it, he parked in front of their house.

GRANDPA

It wasn't kids. It was probably the road. Those spikes the British put in to slow down the Nazis.

ZAKARIYA

Who never came.

GRANDPA

Does he have a spare tire?

KOKAB

Yes but he's wearing his fancy clothes.

GRANDPA

Oh fine, his clothes.

KOKAB

I was trying to make sure he didn't go away mad.

ZAKARIYA

He wasn't that mad.

KOKAB

He was! He got in his car and didn't even notice so he drove off and made it worse.

GRANDPA

Listen, we'll do it. Tofeek has a jack in his old Chevrolet truck.

KOKAB

Oh fine, Tofeek.

SALMA

What.

KOKAB

Oh, Yitzhak is angry, he thinks they did it because he's Jewish so he says things, and your brother Tofeek does not always hold his temper.

                    GRANDPA

No he doesn't.

                    SALMA

I'll deal with Tofeek.

                    ZAKARIYA

Maybe Yitzhak has his own jack.

                    GRANDPA

Maybe so. A couple of old guys will take care of it and protect
Yitzhak's expensive clothes, huh?

                    ZAKARIYA

That's right. We better hurry, it's almost sundown.

                    KOKAB

Thanks Papa, thanks Abu Assad. I'll try to convince him it was those
British spikes.

                    GRANDPA

Good.

                    KOKAB
                    (to Salma)

If it was spikes.

                    ZAKARIYA

I'm sure it was spikes. But we'll take a look.

                    GRANDPA

Come on, kid. If the sun sets, you'll learn how to change a tire.

          (They all go.

          *Noor turns toward us, takes a stance, and starts calling
          out in full volume over our heads as from a rooftop for
          a whole valley to hear:)*

NOOR

Yaaaaaaaaaaaaaaah AHLI BALAD! To all those who can hear this voice. Goooooooooood morning, gooooooood day!

(normal volume, to us)
Rabbi, did I ever tell you I wanted to be the Munadi?

(shouting across the valley)
The water wheel at the flour mill still needs fixing, so the irrigation water from the canaaaaaaaaal will start early.

(normal volume, to us)
I was waiting to grow up and have a big voice so I could climb up on the roof and call out the important events of the day!

> *(The stage is empty still, but Noor remembers the Mediterranean climate of the village which is dry but far from desert. In 1946, when the next scene takes place, the mountainside and valley are full of green and fertile fields, some slanted, some terraced, all irrigated by water flowing down through channels from the mountain spring. One of the main channels has gushing water leading to the south end of the village to power the flour mill. Another channel flows through the central village square and gathers in a network of pools and smaller channels.*
>
> *Noor is imagining himself as the Munadi, a village crier who starts every morning by climbing to a rooftop and calling out the important news of the day to the whole village. This Munadi is on a rooftop overlooking this village square, which is a place where people come to carry their water home, often in pottery jars on their heads. Trading, exchanging, sharing ideas, along with weddings, seasonal and holidays festivals and celebrations would take place at the square. The narrow streets are paved with cobblestone and go back to Greek and Roman times.*

As the Munadi, Noor calls in full volume to be heard down the mountainside and even into the valley.)

NOOR

Tomorroooooooooow morning at four, Abu Saaaaami's field.

(Other actors gather at the edge of the stage to supply voices calling out to the Munadi.)

VOICE

Abu Sami at four in the morning?

VOICE

Umm Sami maybe!

(Some of them laugh.)

NOOR

From there it will go to the field of Ibrahiiiiiiiim Al Khalil, then to Yakooooov.

VOICE

Yakov or Yaqub?

NOOR

Yakoooov the Rabbi's cousin first, Yaqub Abu Ramzi later. Yakooov then to Salmaaaaaaan's potato field, then Malkiiii for his beehives, then to Yaquuub Abu Ramzi, from there in each turn down to the valley. Maaaaay Goooood keep you and your family and your fields and flourish your liiiiiives.

(normal volume, to us)

It was what, 1946. So I was 14. My voice was starting to change but still not loud enough.

(shouting across the valley)

Abu Assaaaad can't find his doooonkey!

VOICE

Again?

NOOR

Keep an eye out for Abu Assad's donkey!

SECOND VOICE

His donkey is in my garden eating my kusa!

NOOR

MABROOOOK Abu Assad's donkey has been found!

SECOND VOICE

He better get over here!

NOOR

AND to all those who are in need, single men and women,
good newwwwwwws, someday soon at your house too we
hope, WEDDING! Abu Assad is honored to invite you for his
granddaughter Fattin's wedding to the Ustaz Jamil who is also leaving
us to Beiruuuuuut.

WOMAN

Mabrooooook Ya Fattin! *(ululates)* Lulululululululeeeesh!

NOOR

Ahlaaaaaan Wasahlaaaaaan, ya Fattin, ya Jamil, MABROOOOK!

(normal volume, to us)
But of course I was never Munadi. I never got the chance.

VOICE

What's on the radio?

VOICE

What's on the radio?

VOICE

What's on the radio?

(Music and noise of a party start up. All leave except Noor as music subsides to indicate that it's a block or two away. Noor starts making a few quick changes in clothing to transform himself into a 15-year old young man. From offstage:)

SALMA

Noor!

NOOR

Yes Mom!

(Salma enters with Kokab, who carries an small embroidered pillow. Noor is now in the scene as a young man. From this point on, everyone responds to him in person.)

SALMA

Where's your grandfather?

NOOR

I don't know. He sent me to look for the Rabbi.

KOKAB

He won't be home.

SALMA

Where then?

KOKAB

I don't know. Salma, I'm sorry. Please give them this.

(She hands Salma the pillow.)

SALMA

It's lovely. You worked hard on this. You should give it to them yourself.

KOKAB

They should have it today on their special day.

SALMA

So come to the wedding and give it today! Don't stay away. It won't be right without you.

KOKAB

I can't.

SALMA

You can. You don't have to miss the whole wedding because something happened far away in a city we've never been to. It wasn't you and we know it wasn't you.

KOKAB

You might know that. But some of your people will blame us.

SALMA

What are you talking, my people?

KOKAB

I'm just saying. What will Ghassan say? Or your brother Tofeek? Or your cousin Aisha even? She might not say it to my face but others will hear.

SALMA

A few people might be blockheads but we'll take care of them.

KOKAB

Or maybe there will be too many and you won't be able to control them. Or maybe it's best we just stay away and let this cool down. '

SALMA

It isn't right. You're our neighbors. You're practically Fattin's aunt.

KOKAB

I know. I'm sorry. Some things run deeper.

(Enter a middle-aged man: Tofeek. The others turn and look at him as if expecting him to speak, but he does not. Silence.)

NOOR

Hi Uncle.

TOFEEK

Hi Noor.

KOKAB

Hello Tofeek.

TOFEEK

Hello Kokab.

(Silence.)

SALMA

Listen. Keep this. In a few days, we'll go together to the newlyweds' house and you can give it to Fattin yourself.

KOKAB

If you think that's best.

SALMA

I do.

KOKAB
(takes pillow)

Alright.

I'll be going, Tofeek You won't have to put up with me at your niece's wedding.

TOFEEK
(neutrally)

Hm.

(Kokab waits a beat, then turns and leaves. Salma glares at Tofeek.)

SALMA

That's all you could say?

TOFEEK

I didn't want to argue with your friend.

SALMA

She's going to miss Fattin's wedding.

TOFEEK

Several people are. I was in the square at the party. Shawul and Malki are not there either.

SALMA

That's too bad.

TOFEEK

I might lay low if I were them. It was hundreds of people.

NOOR

What hundreds of people?

SALMA

Never mind.

TOFEEK

Boy deserves to know.

SALMA

Fine. There was some trouble down in Jerusalem.

TOFEEK

He heard that already. (to Noor) Didn't you?

NOOR

I heard about some hotel.

TOFEEK

King David Hotel. A Jewish underground group set a bomb.

NOOR

Why?

TOFEEK

The hotel was a British headquarters.

NOOR

So they were attacking British? Like our revolt?

TOFEEK

It's not like our revolt and it's not just against the British. That Jewish underground wants us gone too. It's not the first time. They set other bombs in Jerusalem and there was one in a market in Haifa.

NOOR

Was Jewish underground the ones we saw?

TOFEEK

No.

SALMA

Saw where?

(Grandpa enters, dressed up in a nice galabiya/robe.)

GRANDPA

Did you find the Rabbi?

NOOR

No.

SALMA

Kokab says he won't be home.

NOOR

I tried to call out but I couldn't go in the synagogue.

SALMA

Why not?

                         NOOR

There's a lock on the gate.

                         SALMA

A lock?

                        GRANDPA

For what?

                         SALMA

They're scared.

                        TOFEEK

Oh they're scared. Because their people set a bomb.

                        GRANDPA

Well we can't have a wedding until we find the Rabbi. Noor, go to Abu
Jamil's house and tell him to wait.

                         NOOR

Wait how long?

                        GRANDPA

Just tell him to wait. The bride's not ready yet.

                         NOOR

Okay.

                        GRANDPA

And don't stop for kenafeh.

                         NOOR

I don't eat kenafeh.

                        GRANDPA

Wait a minute. What?

                         SALMA

He doesn't eat kenafeh.

GRANDPA

I've seen him eat a whole tray of kenafeh.

SALMA

Not anymore. It's not kosher.

GRANDPA

Are you still playing kosher?

SALMA

He is.

GRANDPA

Well so what? There's no pork in kenafeh.

NOOR

I ate eggs this morning.

GRANDPA

So what?

NOOR

Kenafeh has cheese.

GRANDPA

So what?

NOOR

I can't eat meat and milk this close together.

GRANDPA

What meat and milk? Eggs are not meat.

NOOR

Sure they are.

GRANDPA

Oh, be serious, not even Moses would keep that kind of kosher.

NOOR

It's healthy. Good for the body and soul.

SALMA

When you cook for yourself, you can cook one meal for your body
and one for your soul.

GRANDPA

Listen to your mother. Or go ahead starve yourself, be the first kid in
history to say no to kenafeh. Is the Rabbi making you do this?

NOOR

I read about it in a book.

GRANDPA

A book from the Rabbi. I'm gonna break his head. What are you
waiting for? Get over to Abu Jamil's house.

NOOR

Okay.

(Noor runs off.)

TOFEEK

I wouldn't come to a party today if I was them.

GRANDPA

What, we should cancel the wedding?

TOFEEK

Fine with me. What's the rush?

SALMA

Jamil is leaving for Lebanon.

TOFEEK

Which is just fine, marry your daughter and leave the next day for
Lebanon.

SALMA

Jamil is good for Fattin and she wants him.

GRANDPA

He'll come back with a degree and help the whole village.

TOFEEK

Fine, another book boy.

GRANDPA

A book boy is good.

TOFEEK

Your granddaughter deserves better.GRANDPA

(to Salma)

Would you tell your brother to stop being a donkey.

SALMA

Tofeek, stop being a donkey.

GRANDPA

What she said. Were you talking to the boy about Jerusalem?

TOFEEK

Course I was.

GRANDPA

He's a kid.

TOFEEK

He's old enough. He knows more than you think. Everybody's
dancing like nothing's wrong. I've been trying to tell you but now
hotels are blowing up and the kibbutzim are having target practice
with their British rifles.

GRANDPA

So what? Yitzhak has given some boys his dangerous toys.

TOFEEK

They're not just boys and it's not just Yitzhak. It's the British and they took all our weapons away and they're giving new weapons to the kibbutz. If I were the Rabbi I would hide away too.

GRANDPA

Those boys and their guns are not the same as our Rabbi. He refused to take guns from Yitzhak. In the kibbutz they're from Europe, they bring what they know from Europe, we're different here.

TOFEEK

So what do we do, just wait till they come?

GRANDPA

Or do what instead?

TOFEEK

Get in my truck and go to Damascus and bring back something to defend ourselves.

GRANDPA

Fine. Go to Damascus and stay there, will you? You still have that old pistol? Take it with you.

SALMA

Ammi.

GRANDPA

Do you hear him?

SALMA

I hear him, I hear you, please, both of you. Tofeek. I know it's a bad day, but it's Fattin's day, it's her wedding. Ammi, it's hard, Tofeek's right, the news is bad. But it's Fattin's wedding. My only daughter. Please.

GRANDPA

Alright alright, listen. The British are giving them guns, and they'll stop us if we try to get them. You think they won't know if you go to Damascus? We tried. And look what happened. I don't know what they're going to do, but I do know this: bring guns to our village, you're inviting the trouble. You're bringing it here. All I know is we've got to keep it away from us. If we can. That's all I know. Let's not be the ones to start the trouble here, huh? I'm not your father, but what do you say?

(Pause.)

TOFEEK

Fine.

All I can say is, I hope you're right..

I hope the day doesn't come when we face them with their guns.

and us with nothing but empty hands.

(Noor runs on.)

NOOR

I told Abu Jamil.

GRANDPA

What did he say?

NOOR

He wonders what's going on but he'll wait.

GRANDPA
(aggravated)
Annh. Did you see the Rabbi anywhere?

NOOR

No.

GRANDPA

Dammit. Aaaaanh, I know where he is, he makes my head hurt. I'll be back in a little while.

NOOR

Where do you think he is?

SALMA

At the cave?

GRANDPA

Yeah.

NOOR

The Zohar Cave?

GRANDPA

Yes, the Zohar Cave, why does he go there, he knows I don't like it..

NOOR

Can I come?

GRANDPA

No. Go eat some lamb.

NOOR

Grandpa, it's not kosher. They cook it in the mother's milk.

GRANDPA

Fucking Rabbi. Alright, come on.

(*They start off but Tofeek stops them.*)

TOFEEK

Good, go hunt him down, I'm gonna go find some arak to drink and then I'm gonna go dance the dabkeh, because that's what we do on a day like this, right? Like nothing happened, huh?

(*He goes.*)

NOOR

What was that about?

(*Grandpa shakes head and they walk away, with Salma leaving opposite after Tofeek. Music and party noise fade and out.*

Grandpa and Noor start walking in a wide circle. They

are walking up a hill through the wild oak and carob
trees outside the village. After a while:)

NOOR

Does he always go up to the cave?

GRANDPA

Today is not always. But yes. Sometimes.

NOOR

Grandpa?

GRANDPA

What?

NOOR

Have you been to the kibbutz at Jermoun?

GRANDPA
(stops, looks at him)

What about it?

NOOR
(hesitates)

Tofeek took me there. In his truck.

GRANDPA

When?

NOOR

On the way to the market at Saffad. At Jermoun they have those rifles.

GRANDPA
(shaking head, grimly)

Yes I've been by it. Why did he take you there?

NOOR

Don't get mad at him. I asked him to.

GRANDPA

You did?!

NOOR

You never want to talk about it and I wanted to see. They're not just boys. They're men and there's women too. They have uniforms. They crawl under wires and up over walls and they shoot at targets. It's like those photographs of soldiers from the war.

(*Grandpa looks at him, then starts walking and Noor follows.*)

GRANDPA

I'm sorry he took you there.

NOOR

I know you don't like talking about it. But Jermoun is just across the valley

GRANDPA

I don't like talking about it right now, that's for sure. (*points off*) You see that rock?

NOOR

Yeah?

GRANDPA

That's Ghazal's rock.

NOOR

Ghazal who?

GRANDPA

Ghazal Kenaan. They found him here with his blood on that rock. He went off to fight in the revolt against the British. He was a strong boy. He could wrestle a bear. What a stupid waste. Like your dad. Your dad who's not going to be at his daughter's wedding today. So no I don't want to talk about it. Can we just find this Rabbi so we can have a wedding for your sister? (*points ahead*) Here.

(Zakariya has entered and is sitting upstage on the ground with his back to them, some distance. He is in the cave. Grandpa and Noor have walked a wide circle and are approaching him. Grandpa stops a little ways away.)

GRANDPA

There's the cave. Go see if he's there.

NOOR

Me?

GRANDPA

It hurts my neck getting in. Go ahead.

(Noor steps closer, kneels down to look inside and see Zakariya inside the small cave. Zakariya doesn't turn to see him. Noor doesn't know what to do. He stays kneeling by the imagined entrance to the cave.)

NOOR

He's here.

(Grandpa speaks from where he stands outside the cave.)

GRANDPA

Well tell him my granddaughter is ready and Jamil's dad is ready and the priest, the imam, and the mukhtar are all ready to come to my house. Everyone's ready except my neighbor the Rabbi. Who seems to be hiding out in an old cave. Ask him, what, is he afraid all of a sudden?

(Pause. Noor starts uncertainly.)

NOOR

Grandpa wants to know if –

ZAKARIYA

I hear him. *(louder)* Maybe a little. Mainly sad.

123

                              NOOR

He says —

                            GRANDPA

Because of what his Jewish pals did?

              (The whole conversation takes place as if in separate
              rooms with Noor kneeling between them.)

                            ZAKARIYA

They're not my pals. Stern Gang crazies. Went through awful things
in Europe but now they come here and start blowing up buildings.
We're not in Europe. What's everyone saying at the wedding?

                            GRANDPA

They're pissed off.

                            ZAKARIYA

They should be. I am too. The Torah says not to commit murder. It's
not one of those complicated rules. Just says: don't do it.

                            GRANDPA

So what are you gonna do? You can't stay up here forever. I got sick of
it after three months.

                              NOOR

What?

                            GRANDPA

What what, you think only Rabbis hide in this cave?

                              NOOR

You hid here?

                            ZAKARIYA

Who was it, the Turks?

                            GRANDPA

Yeah.

ZAKARIYA

The Turks drafted your Grandpa to fight in the Great War.

NOOR

Grandpa was in the Great War?

GRANDPA

Only till I could get out. I bribed a Turkish sergeant and I never knew my heels could touch my butt till I ran that fast.

ZAKARIYA

But the Turks were already here in the village.

GRANDPA

So I hid in this cave three months till they were gone. I had a stiff neck for a year.

ZAKARIYA

Lot of people have hid in this cave. From Alexander the Great and from Romans and Persians and Crusaders and Turks and British.

GRANDPA

Hey remember Sami?

ZAKARIYA

Yeah.

NOOR

Sami? What about him?

GRANDPA

Years back. Sami was part of one of those Jewish underground groups. The British were chasing him and he came here to hide.

NOOR

Wait – Sami isn't Jewish. He's a sheikh.

GRANDPA

Because we brought him down and gave him some clothes and

when the British came looking for Jewish underground, we
called him "Sheikh". "Hello Sheikh", "Have you seen any Jewish
underground, ya Sheikh?" So he was safe. He's been Sheikh Sami
ever since.

NOOR

Sheikh Sami is really Jewish?

ZAKARIYA

I think he's forgotten. He never comes to synagogue.

GRANDPA

We should remind him sometime. His name was . . . what?

ZAKARIYA

I don't remember . . . Natan.

GRANDPA

Natan.

NOOR

Wow.

ZAKARIYA

This has been a safe place for lots of people.

NOOR

Did my dad hide here?

(Silence.)

NOOR

Before the British got him?

(Silence.)

GRANDPA

Enough of this talk. Shall we call off the wedding? Abu Jamil is
waiting with his son. I need you beside me. Fattin doesn't have a dad
to stand with her, it takes at least two of us to take his place. Come
stand with me, will you?

ZAKARIYA

You think it's okay?

GRANDPA

If it's not okay for somebody there, what will we do, Kosher Boy?

NOOR

Break some heads?

GRANDPA

That's right. Jerusalem is far. You coming?

ZAKARIYA

Have they got kenafeh?

GRANDPA

The best, all the way from Nablus
But hey: did you have eggs for breakfast?

ZAKARIYA

Yeah, Kokab made some –

GRANDPA

Uhp! No kenafe for you.

ZAKARIYA

What no kenafe?

GRANDPA

Chief Rabbi Noor says it's not kosher.

ZAKARIYA

What? Not kosher why?

NOOR

Eggs and cheese. It's in a little book you have.

ZAKARIYA

Well, I'll tell you.

(Zakariya pulls himself up, bends down as he leaves the little cave. Noor does the same. They stand up outside.)

ZAKARIYA

Whoever wrote that book never tasted kenafeh. Listen.

GRANDPA

What?

ZAKARIYA

I'll come and stand with you and Fattin at your house when they come to take her to Jamil.

GRANDPA

Good.

ZAKARIYA

And then you go off to the wedding. And I'll go home.

GRANDPA

Why?

ZAKARIYA

Standing beside you is fine. I just don't want to talk to everyone else today. Tell them I'm sick.

GRANDPA

They know you're not sick.

ZAKARIYA

This is all I can do today.

GRANDPA

Alright alright, we'll say you ate too much kenafeh. It was because of the pork.

(big sigh)

Everything has to happen on this day.

(Grandpa stands, looking far off. Noor and Zakariya join him.)

NOOR

What are you looking at?

GRANDPA

(gestures with his chin)
There it is. Jermoun. Across the valley like you said. You see it?

NOOR

Yeah.

GRANDPA

So they're practicing with their British rifles now.

ZAKARIYA

A few of them.

NOOR

Not just a few.

GRANDPA

No. Tofeek is right. Not so few.
And now Noor has seen them. I wish you hadn't.

NOOR

They'd be there anyway, Grandpa.

(Silence.)

GRANDPA

You know that used to be Saleh's land.

ZAKARIYA

Yeah.

GRANDPA

Olives and figs and almonds. He kept some sheep.

ZAKARIYA

Where is Saleh now?

GRANDPA

In Jaffa. He's a streetcleaner.

NOOR

What happened?

GRANDPA

Some Jews showed up one day with a bill of sale from a Turkish landlord Saleh never heard of.

NOOR

They can't do that.

GRANDPA

They did it and the British backed them up. They built the kibbutz and Saleh's in Jaffa sweeping streets. His brother had to go too and now he's in a cigarette factory.

(Silence while they look.)

GRANDPA

I'm glad he's not here. I wouldn't want him to be standing here looking at what used to be his.

ZAKARIYA

Those people in Jermoun are still new here. Europe was different. They're not used to how we do things here. Give them time, they'll come to understand.

GRANDPA

Will they give Saleh back his fields?

(Silence.)

GRANDPA

Noor. After the wedding.

NOOR

Yeah?

GRANDPA

I don't know who you usually run off with, but don't tonight. Tonight you come with me.

NOOR

What for?

GRANDPA

Just do it. After the wedding you come with me.

(*They go off.*

Salma enters, walks forward to face audience, gazes down at something in front of her. She kneels on the ground, making herself comfortable, as if talking to someone sitting on the ground in front of her. It's a quiet place at the edge of the village.)

SALMA

Fattin got married today, my love. To Jamil, just as you said she would. He's a lovely boy. He finished school and he's going away to university in Beirut, which is not so nice for a while but he'll be back. Your daughter was so happy and so beautiful ...

(*It is too much and she can't talk for a moment. She collects herself.*)

SALMA

She doesn't like all that sitting and being stared at. You didn't either, remember? But it was still glorious. All day long she would catch me across the room with her beautiful eyes and I always knew exactly what she meant. Sometimes it was "I'm so happy, Momma" and sometimes it was "Am I beautiful enough, Momma?" But every time, no matter what else, every time and always, she was also saying to me: "Papa. Papa's with me, Papa's in my heart. I wish Papa was here." It was so lovely seeing you in her eyes. I had to look away sometimes. It was too wonderful, it was too much.

(She can't talk for a moment.)

SALMA

There was some trouble in Jerusalem and it kept some of our friends away. That was too bad.

I wish you could meet your son now. He's a fine boy. You can be proud of him. He still reads books, just as you said he would. It's a headache though, because the books make him decide he's Christian, and now he thinks he's Jewish and we don't know what to feed him. We don't let him read Sheikh Spear because who knows, he might decide he's British and then we'd have to throw him out.

He also thinks he's really good at hiding. But he's not. He's terrible at it. I don't know why he keeps trying.

Come on then. Come sit here.

(Enter Noor and Grandpa. They kneel beside her.)

GRANDPA

Noor thought that you might like to be alone for a while.

SALMA
(nods)

That was kind of him. But you're not so good at hiding either. And you're welcome here with me.

(They are silent, looking at the grave.)

SALMA

So Tofeek took you to see what they're doing at Jermoun.

NOOR

Yeah.

SALMA

And your Grandpa was mad about it.

GRANDPA

I wasn't —

SALMA

Your Grandpa was annoyed about it. Your Grandpa gets annoyed at Tofeek a lot.

GRANDPA

He can be annoying.

SALMA

He can. Especially when he feels bad himself. *(to Noor)* Your uncle Tofeek thinks he talked your Dad into joining the Revolt against the British. I think your Dad would have joined no matter what. But Tofeek thinks he was responsible, and your Grandfather thinks so too.

GRANDPA

I don't think that.

SALMA

Yes you do. Even when you know better.

(to Noor)

And somehow your Dad got taken by the British and Tofeek didn't. And Tofeek blames himself. So I wish your Grandpa would give him a break sometimes. And you too, Noor.

NOOR

Okay.

SALMA

You should know something. Rabbi Zakariya was a great help during that time. When your dad was gone and the harvest was coming and we didn't know what we would do. The Rabbi was right there with us. *(to Grandpa)* Isn't that right?

GRANDPA

That's right. Not much of a farmer but always there to help . . .

SALMA

Oh stop. *(to Noor)* Others too, from the synagogue. Malki even left his bees to come help us. Showul still comes sometimes. I know it was confusing today, with that bad news from Jerusalem. But you should remember that when we really needed it, the whole village was your father.

(Pause.)

SALMA

Did you know that your grandfather doesn't come here?

NOOR

No.

SALMA

He hasn't come here since it happened. Isn't that right?

(Grandpa nods.)

SALMA

But he decided that today was the day.
Isn't that right?

(Grandpa nods. He's staring at the grave, holding himself together. He lifts his chin to point at it.)

GRANDPA

Your dad had a big heart. It made him smart, it made him brave. He wanted things to be better so he went off. I didn't like it but we tried it his way. My one son. Maybe I haven't forgiven him either.
But I wish he was sitting here now instead of me.

(He can't talk for a moment.)

GRANDPA

He's not though.
And we need to know that you understand.
We have a choice.
If there's trouble, we can choose that it won't start here. We can choose that we won't be the ones to start it.

SALMA

We know it's hard. We know your friends see them over in Jermoun
with their guns. And they talk about doing that themselves. But
listen. Remember what happened to your dad. And remember.
Everyone in this village is family

GRANDPA

That's how we do it here. Everyone here is family. And we don't want
to lose anyone. Ever again. Huh?

(Noor nods slowly.
They're silent.)

SALMA

Okay then.
Maybe enough here for now.

(She rises. Looks at Grandpa, who does not.)

SALMA

You want to stay a little?

(Grandpa pauses. Then starts to get up.)

GRANDPA

I'll come with you.

*(Grandpa and Salma start to move away but stop
when Noor speaks.)*

NOOR

But Grandpa.

(They turn to look at him.)

NOOR

Jermoun is close
What do we do if they come here?

(Pause.)

GRANDPA

I guess we just have to hope. That Jermoun has mothers and grandfathers too. And they don't want to lose anyone either. Let's go, huh?

(Noor pauses a moment. Then rises and they leave together.)

Sound: the buzz of a static-filled radio broadcast of male voices which we can't quite understand.

Zakariya enters, stands listening to the broadcast.

Tofeek enters, stand beside the Rabbi, listens as well.

Tofeek has a handful of seeds which he's eating. Without looking, he holds out hand. Without looking, Zakariya reaches over and takes some from Tofeek's hand. They and others have stood this way innumerable times, sharing seeds and snacks; so often that they don't need to look at the snacks or each other. They stand side by side eating seeds and listening.)

TOFEEK

Partition.

ZAKARIYA
(nods a little, slowly)

Partition.

TOFEEK

Partition my ass.
Fucking British.
Scuse my mouth.

ZAKARIYA

Americans too.

TOFEEK

Maybe we'll end up in Haifa. By the beach.

ZAKARIYA

You know how to swim?

(Tofeek doesn't respond.)

ZAKARIYA

Me neither.

TOFEEK

Mm.
Partition my ass.

ZAKARIYA

Yeah.
Mine too.

(He and Tofeek share a chuckle.
Pause.)

TOFEEK

See you at Passover.
Or maybe we won't, huh?

(Tofeek wanders off while the Rabbi keeps listening.
Radio noise subsides and goes out. From opposite,
Noor enters behind and sits. He has changed clothes;
over a year has passed.)

NOOR

What does it mean?

ZAKARIYA

Partition. Parting in two.

(Zakariya turns, enters a new scene with Noor, goes to
sit with Noor as if they have already been talking.)

                    NOOR

Everything?

                  ZAKARIYA

I guess.

                    NOOR

What, the air?

                  ZAKARIYA

If they could, maybe the air.

                    NOOR

The water?

                  ZAKARIYA

Probably the water.

                    NOOR

Half here, half there?

                  ZAKARIYA

Like Moses parted the Red Sea.

                    NOOR

Sure, if they had Moses. What about the basateen, the fields and
gardens?

                  ZAKARIYA

Not sure.

                    NOOR

Just in half? Grandpa said that his field is ten times bigger than yours.

                  ZAKARIYA

It's not every field, I don't think. It's the whole country.

                    NOOR

The whole country? Like we're here and you're there? With a wall
between us?

ZAKARIYA

Not sure, maybe a fence.

NOOR

Who did this "partition" thing, anyway? They say the United Nations.
What is that?

ZAKARIYA

They're new. They sit in America, New York.

NOOR

They sit in America and do partition from there?

ZAKARIYA

They have good maps.

NOOR

How good are the maps? Do they show that your house and our
house are stuck together?

ZAKARIYA

Not sure about that.

NOOR

Do they know that we drink from the same spring?

ZAKARIYA

I doubt they know about this one.

NOOR

They probably don't even have a water spring like us. They have
faucets inside their houses. They turn the faucet this way and water
comes out.

ZAKARIYA

Yeah, that would be nice, huh? I wouldn't have to ask you to carry the
water for me all the time.

NOOR

I don't mind it. Anytime you need water just call me. When Grandpa
heard this partition he went crazy.

ZAKARIYA

What did he say?

NOOR

He said, "What, Palestine is a loaf of bread? You can cut it with a knife?"

ZAKARIYA
(chuckles)

Loaf of bread.

NOOR

"How do you split us up from the Jews? Our houses share a wall,
for thousands of years, why now? And the fucking British! And
the Turks."

ZAKARIYA

And the Jews?

NOOR

No. He didn't say that.

ZAKARIYA

What about your grandmother?

NOOR

She said "This country will only be liberated — "

NOOR & ZAKARIYA

By the Russians.

ZAKARIYA

Yep. That's her.

NOOR

Ammi. What's really gonna happen?

ZAKARIYA

I don't know. There might be trouble but we've made it through
trouble before. We can hope this will just blow over us. Like the
Persians and the Romans and the Turks, and now even the British.
We might have to go hide in a cave for a while, but then we'll come
back and we'll still be here. As always.

*(They start to leave together, but Noor leaves while
Zakariya turns away to go to a different spot.*

*Two chairs are set at opposite sides of the stage.
Zakariya sits at one side with Kokab at the opposite
side. An upcoming scene will take place simultaneously
on the stage between them.*

*Despite the formal arrangement, they speak as if sitting
in a room together. Both are deeply disturbed.)*

KOKAB

So you want to give them all we have.

ZAKARIYA

Not all we have. Don't be quarrelsome.

KOKAB

What then?

ZAKARIYA

Everyone's giving them something, we can too.

KOKAB

Our people at the camp need more than we have.

ZAKARIYA

These people are hungry. They've walked all this way, they're up on
the mountain and they don't have anything.

KOKAB

Our people at the camp don't have anything. Lots of people are hungry. There's trouble.

ZAKARIYA

This wasn't just trouble.

KOKAB

Fighting then.

ZAKARIYA

It wasn't just fighting. It wasn't soldiers, it wasn't a shootout. It was people, just people. I'm scared.

KOKAB

We're all scared.

ZAKARIYA

You don't understand. I'm scared of us.

(Pause.)

ZAKARIYA

Those people who came here are Arabs from Qisarya. They walked all the way here from Qisarya.

KOKAB

They say they did.

ZAKARIYA

What, you think they're making it up? They walked all the way from Qisarya.

(Grandpa and Salma have entered, standing upstage separately from Zakariya or Kokab. They are in a separate scene from Zakariya and Kokab, though they share the stage. They speak out toward us as they ask questions of the Arabs from Qisarya, whom we do not see. Zakariya continues to describe and narrate what the Arabs from Qisarya are saying to them. Grandpa

*and Salma do not respond to Zakariya or Kokab, nor
do Zakariya or Kokab respond to them.)*

SALMA

How many are you?

ZAKARIYA

Seven or eight families, they said.

GRANDPA

Is that all?

ZAKARIYA

Others escaped in other directions. They live by the sea. One man
says he was in his fishing boat. He heard shooting, he went running
back.

GRANDPA

Soldiers?

ZAKARIYA

Not soldiers, the man said. We knew them, he said. They were
neighbors. Jewish customers, from the kibbutz at Sdot Yam. They
come buy vegetables and fish, now they come with their guns,
running around shooting their machine guns in the air. They point
their guns and they round up all the Arabs in Qisarya.

KOKAB

What for?

ZAKARIYA

That's the thing. They push all the Arabs inside an old monastery,
they crowd everyone in there. And then the Arabs hear an
explosion and another explosion, and explosions and explosions,
on and on. And then they let everyone out. And these Jewish
neighbors with their machine guns, they kept pointing them and
they told all the Arabs to start walking. In one long line. Out of
the village to the main road away. And then they saw, the man said

they saw that the village was covered in a cloud of dust, and all the homes were demolished to rubble. All the wheat and the crops were burnt.

GRANDPA

Just blow up everything?

SALMA

Why?

ZAKARIYA

No one knows why. Why would they do that? He asked them where are we going? And the Jewish neighbors with their guns said Anywhere. Just don't come back. There's nothing for you here.

GRANDPA

Where were the British?

ZAKARIYA

The British stood there watching, the man said. The British just stood there watching.

GRANDPA

We'll get you some warm clothes and blankets.

SALMA

Some bread and labaneh as well.

GRANDPA

You should come down and stay with us here.

ZAKARIYA

A woman said You're very kind, but we'll stay up on the mountain.
It's safer. We have to move on.
The man said You should get ready.
They kept saying that.
They're coming here too. Sooner or later.
You should get ready yourselves.

*(Grandpa and Salma stare at the invisible speakers,
disturbed; then turn and leave.)*

KOKAB

One incident then.

ZAKARIYA

It wasn't just one.
They met others already on the road.
From Balad al-Shaykh. From Wadi Rushmayya in Haifa. From Lifta.
From others we haven't heard about yet.
Why burn all the wheat and destroy all the homes?
It's not just war.
What kind of war is this?

KOKAB

There have been riots on both sides.

ZAKARIYA

This wasn't a riot! It was Jewish neighbors driving away other neighbors.

KOKAB

We can't feed everyone who comes through here with a story.

ZAKARIYA

It's not just a story! You think they made it all up?

KOKAB

I don't know.

ZAKARIYA

And walked all the way from Qisarya for nothing? What about the other places?

KOKAB

We don't know. They exaggerate sometimes. We have reason to be afraid too.

ZAKARIYA

Is that why our Ezra is up on his roof with a rifle at night? Is the rifle from Yitzhak?

KOKAB

I don't know. It might be from Jermoun.

ZAKARIYA

Those were from Yitzhak. Or someone like Yitzhak.

KOKAB

It's not safe here anymore.

ZAKARIYA

We're as safe here as we've always been.

KOKAB

Safe like our people were safe before the massacre in Hebron?

ZAKARIYA

Our people do things too. Those bombs in Jerusalem and Haifa. But this is different. Qisarya was not just fighting back and forth. It's like those Jews from the kibbutz were seeing what they could get away with. And the British just stood there —

KOKAB
(rises suddenly)
Papa. You're the one who needs to understand.
We need to take care of our own people now.

(She turns and leaves.

Zakariya sits, staring out past us.

Enter Noor at the other side of the stage in a separate scene with Grandpa and Salma following.)

NOOR

It's not fair.

GRANDPA

I'm sorry, Noor.

NOOR

Some people come here, they tell us stories, we're not part of this whatever it is.

GRANDPA

We are.

SALMA

Qisarya is not so far.

NOOR

It's all the way to the sea.

GRANDPA

Lots of things are not fair these days. I'm sorry, Noor. This is how it has to be.

NOOR

It's almost sundown. What will he do without a Shabbat helper?

GRANDPA

He'll be fine. He'll light the lamp before sundown. If he needs special help, I'll be right here next door.

NOOR

It's not right. I'm going.

GRANDPA
(stands in front of him)

Noor.

NOOR
(tries to step around him)

It's not right.

GRANDPA

Do what I tell you.

SALMA

Noor.

(Noor stops. Silence.)

GRANDPA

People are angry. Young ones don't understand. After Qisarya, they don't like to see a young man acting like a servant.

NOOR

I'm not a servant, I'm a friend.

GRANDPA

I know, but things have changed. I don't like it either. It's only for a while. I already told him. I'm sorry.

(Grandpa and Salma leave in different directions.

Noor stays, silent.

Kokab returns her side of the stage. She has two cloth bags.)

KOKAB

Here. *(sets them down in front of her)* We can spare this much.

ZAKARIYA

Thanks. Thank you.

KOKAB

You can give it to your Shabbat helper when he comes.

(Pause.)

ZAKARIYA

He won't be coming.
Not anymore. For a while.

(Silence.)

KOKAB

I'm sorry.
I'm sure he's disappointed too.

(pause)

Maybe it's for the best.
Maybe we weren't such good neighbors after all.

*(She leaves.
Noor stands, Zakariya sits. They are on the same stage
but isolated from each other in two different locations.)*

ZAKARIYA

What kind of war is this?

NOOR

I don't understand.
What kind of war is this?

end act one

ACT TWO

(*Zakariya walks on with an empty bucket. He walks to center, sets the bucket down and leans it over almost horizontally, letting it fill from the invisible stream.*

Zakariya is at the village square where one channel of water from the spring is kept free for drinking water. He is too old to lift a pottery jar full of water onto his head as the women of the village do. He is therefore making do with a metal bucket which has a carrying handle.

Winter has passed and it is warm springtime now.

Noor enters upstage behind him, stops, watches him.

Zakariya, not seeing Noor, tries to pick up the full bucket, finds it too heavy. He pours some water out and tries again to lift it. Zakariya dumps more water out of the bucket. He sits to rest.)

NOOR

Would it be easier if it came out of a faucet in your house?

ZAKARIYA
(*turns to see him*)

A faucet?

NOOR

Yeah.

ZAKARIYA

Not for me.

NOOR

Why not?

ZAKARIYA

I like my water straight from the mouth of the spring. Even if I have to give up the bucket and come here to drink when I get thirsty.

(Pause.)

NOOR

I guess I can't walk over and carry that bucket for you.

ZAKARIYA

No. Best not. Not in the village square. Your Grandpa and the others are right. Things have changed. For the time being, at least.

(Silence.

Noor finds a place to sit, some distance away.)

NOOR

You think all the stories are true?

ZAKARIYA

I don't know.

NOOR

In Haifa? Jewish soldiers rolling barrels of explosives down the hills on people? Driving them into the sea?

ZAKARIYA

I don't know. I don't think they're making it up.

NOOR

And Jewish soldiers massacring people in Sassa and Deir Yassin.

ZAKARIYA

I don't know. We need to get through this.

(Pause.)

NOOR

What do you do on Shabbat?

ZAKARIYA

God will forgive an old man for making his own tea.
Probably not good to be here chatting too long.

NOOR

We're still allowed to talk, I think.
I was waiting for you.

ZAKARIYA

Why?

NOOR

To ask about Kokab. And the rest.

ZAKARIYA

Oh.

NOOR

We saw them leave. All your people. Kokab too?

ZAKARIYA

Yeah.

NOOR

They wouldn't even talk to us. Did everybody go?

ZAKARIYA

Pretty much. Avram and David Minasheh and Dvorah Sadoodeh and
the others. They're all hearing stories about Arab armies from Syria
and Jordan.

NOOR

Where did they go?

ZAKARIYA

Tiberias. Tabariya. Kokab thought it would be safer for those Jewish
immigrants she's trying to help. She asked Yosi if maybe one or two
of our people could come along to help, and before you know it, the
whole congregation decided Tabariya sounded safer.

NOOR

Because the British took all the Arabs out??

ZAKARIYA

I guess so.

NOOR

What about you?

ZAKARIYA

She wanted me to come too.

NOOR

But you didn't go.

ZAKARIYA
(shaking head)

My place is here, not Tabariya.

NOOR

When are they coming back?

ZAKARIYA

Don't know. She said it would just be a few days.

NOOR

Did anybody stay?

ZAKARIYA

Sheikh Sami.

NOOR

Because he forgot he's Jewish?

ZAKARIYA

Everybody else went. I don't know if they're my congregation anymore. Maybe they're Kokab's.

NOOR

Maybe Sami will come to synagogue now.

ZAKARIYA

That would be thoughtful of him.

NOOR

He's the only one who stayed?

ZAKARIYA

A few others. Malki won't leave his honey bees. Shmoal is too old to go anywhere. I'll have to check in on him. Couple others to watch over the fields. But all the rest went. They think it's only for a little while.

NOOR

If they don't want to live here, they don't have to.

ZAKARIYA

They're just afraid.

NOOR

Of what? Us? They're the ones who pushed Arabs in Haifa into the sea.

ZAKARIYA

It wasn't our people here who did that.

NOOR

Their people in Haifa did.

(Pause.)

NOOR

I wish I was in Haifa when it happened.

ZAKARIYA

I'm glad you were not.

NOOR

I should have been there helping them fight instead of sitting here safe.
I told my mom and my grandpa that I would not.
But things have changed.
I should have been there helping them fight.

(Pause.)

ZAKARIYA

I'm glad you were not.

You think you'd fight.

But maybe you'd wake up to bombing.

And your grandmother would trip and fall.

And you'd have to help her or help somebody else.

And your sister or somebody's sister would get separated in the rush
and the noise, and you'd have to look for her and try to keep your
family together.

And you'd end up standing in the ocean yourself, hoping there was a
boat and trying to get your sister and mother and grandmother into it
and hoping no one shoots you because you don't have a gun anyway.
Maybe it would be like that.

I'm glad you were here and not there.

(Pause. Noor stands, steps over and picks up the bucket.)

ZAKARIYA

Noor, stop it. Don't.

NOOR

It's okay.

ZAKARIYA

No it's not.

NOOR

I'm helping an old man with a bucket. Why should anyone complain?

ZAKARIYA

They won't complain to you. It's your mother and your grandfather
and your family. They'll get the trouble. It's okay. I'll be fine.

(Noor pauses, sets the bucket down.)

NOOR

I wish this were over

ZAKARIYA

It will be. God willing.

NOOR

God willing.

> *(Noor goes.*
> *Pause.*
>
> *Zakariya lifts the heavy bucket, turns and leaves.*
>
> *Grandpa enters, speaks toward us.)*

GRANDPA

You didn't see them. You wouldn't argue if you saw them.
I've gone to the market in Saffad every Sunday since I was fourteen.
Now I go and I find a line of people.
There is no market at Saffad, old man.
A thousand Jewish troops came with good British weapons. All the
Arabs are gone from Saffad. Turn around, old man.
How do I feed my family now?
I gave them some bread. And they said that thing.
They're coming.
You should get ready, old man.
They will come here next.

> *(Enter Tofeek to stand beside him. They speak as if*
> *continuing their conversation.)*

TOFEEK

I know it's hard. We'll take care of your family, no matter what. But
some of us will stay here, no matter what.

> *(Grandpa turns attention to Tofeek. Though no one*
> *else happens to be there, they are in a public square of*
> *the village.)*

GRANDPA

Tofeek, it's Saffad, do you understand? One mountain away. The Jewish army has taken Qisarya to the west of us, Tabariya to the east, Deir Yassin down by Jerusalem, and now they have taken Saffad just to the north. They are all around us and they are on their way here. None of us want to go, but it's time.

TOFEEK

I don't care how close Saffad is.

GRANDPA

Think about the kids, will you? It will only be for a few days.

TOFEEK

Go if you want. Some of us will stay.

GRANDPA

They have an army, we don't. What are you gonna, defend the village with your rusty pistol?

TOFEEK

If I have to. If it's all we have.

GRANDPA

Don't you know why the British left you that gun?

TOFEEK

Cuz I hid it.

GRANDPA

Cuz they knew it was too rusty to shoot.

TOFEEK

Not like the ones they gave the Jews anyway.

(Enter Salma and Noor.)

SALMA

Ammi, it's no good.

NOOR

Abu Jamil won't listen.

SALMA

It's his son, we can't persuade him. I tried, Fattin tried, he won't come with us if we don't find Jamil.

GRANDPA

Annnnnh, what a pain in the head. We'll just have to go find him.

SALMA

How?

GRANDPA

I'll go.

SALMA

To Tabariya?

TOFEEK

What, on your donkey? I'll go. I've got my truck.

GRANDPA

The old Chevrolet?

TOFEEK

It's not so old.

GRANDPA

You'll need a lot of gas.

TOFEEK

I have a full tank. And half the way is downhill. I'll put it in neutral.

GRANDPA

We might have to fish you out of the lake.

SALMA

And the way back is uphill.

TOFEEK

I have enough gas, don't worry.

GRANDPA

You don't even like Jamil.

TOFEEK

IIIII like him. Enough to bring him back from a prison camp. He's
Fattin's husband, it ought to be me.

GRANDPA

You'll just lose your temper and find somebody to fight and get killed.

NOOR

I'll go.

SALMA

No.

GRANDPA

You're just a kid.

NOOR

I'm not.

ZAKARIYA
(starting offstage, speaking as he enters)
Oooooor else maybe, you could ask your neighbor.

TOFEEK

Look who's here.

ZAKARIYA

Hello Neighbor.

GRANDPA

Hello Rabbi.

ZAKARIYA

We don't talk much anymore and I know I might not be welcome. But you're standing out here shouting I couldn't help hear. Why do you need to go to Tabariya?

TOFEEK

Might not be your business.

SALMA

Tofeek, he's offering to help.

TOFEEK

We don't need his help.

GRANDPA

We might. *(to Zakariya)* It's Jamil. He was trying to come back from Lebanon and the Jewish soldiers took him prisoner. We think he's at the prison camp in Tabariya.

ZAKARIYA

And his dad won't leave without him.

GRANDPA

Right.

ZAKARIYA

Well, I hope no one has to leave, but if you need someone to go to Tabariya, you should send someone Jewish. Like me.

TOFEEK

You?

ZAKARIYA

Use your head, Tofeek. I'll be safe. I want to check on Kokab and the rest anyway. I'll be glad to get out and do something useful.

TOFEEK

We'll be fine.

GRANDPA

Tofeek, don't be a donkey. This is about Jamil.

TOFEEK

Alright. But keep away from our spring.

GRANDPA

What?

TOFEEK

The Jews put typhoid in the water at Akka.

SALMA

Tofeek.

GRANDPA

This is our Rabbi and it's his spring too. Apologize.

TOFEEK

Alright alright, I apologize.

ZAKARIYA

Very sincere. How does your wife put up with you?

NOOR

I'll come too.

SALMA

Why you?

NOOR

We can't drive into the city. We'll have to walk, and the Rabbi shouldn't do that by himself. And I can keep an eye on him for Uncle Tofeek.

ZAKARIYA

I don't know about that. It's dangerous.

GRANDPA

It's a ways, old man. Don't go alone.

NOOR

You can tell them I'm your son.

ZAKARIYA

Grandson maybe. Alright.

GRANDPA

Alright. Noor, you don't let anything happen to him.

NOOR

Okay.

GRANDPA

Rabbi, you don't let anything happen to Noor. Stay safe and come back soon. Saffad is close, no matter what this stonehead says.

SALMA

(to Noor)

Be careful when you see Kokab.

NOOR

Why?

SALMA

I don't know. It's like I don't know her anymore.

(to Zakariya)

Bring him back safe, okay?

(They go.

Kokab enters and starts pulling chairs together and spreading blankets over them.

Noor enters behind her.)

KOKAB

Okay, grandson. I guess that makes you my nephew, huh? This is all we have, I'm afraid.

NOOR

It's fine. I appreciate it. I didn't think we were gonna stay the night.

KOKAB

I don't know what Papa was thinking he could do as if by magic. I don't know what he thinks about anything anymore.

NOOR

Is he okay? He's been gone for hours.

KOKAB

He's fine, probably. He's a good man but he's careless sometimes and things fall to other people. Now he thinks he can just walk in and talk to colonels and generals? At least he took off his Arab scarf.

NOOR

It's called a kufiyeh.

KOKAB

Thanks very much for that information.

NOOR

Sorry. Kokab?

KOKAB

Call me Kokhava please.

NOOR

Okay. Kokhava? You don't have to pretend you're my aunt if you don't want.

KOKAB

Too late. He told them you're his grandson, so I better get used to it. I think you're stuck with him. Just like I am.

NOOR

Whose house was this? Do you know?

KOKAB

I don't know. It was empty when we got here.

NOOR

They didn't tell you?

KOKAB

No.

NOOR

Did you look around for anything?

KOKAB

No. Noor. We're just trying to make our way here.

NOOR

What will you do when they come back?

KOKAB
(a beat)

We'll see.

NOOR

Is the prison camp far?

KOKAB

It's not close.

NOOR

I was supposed to make sure he's safe. I should go find him.

KOKAB

You will not! The streets are full of soldiers. You shouldn't have come in the first place, and if you leave this house you will never come back. Go to sleep.

NOOR

They say a lot of miracles happened here.

KOKAB

Yes and the last miracle was you and my father still alive.

NOOR

Lake Tabariya is where Jesus walked on water.

KOKAB

He must've been made of wood.

NOOR

This is also where he fed the hungry. Five loaves of bread and two fish to feed five thousand people.

KOKAB

I could use that miracle right now.

> *(Another woman enters to stand at the side of the stage. She speaks from the side and we realize she is giving voice to an invisible girl. Just as with Noor in the earlier scene, Noor and Kokab respond to the invisible girl as if she were in the scene with them, and they take no notice of the woman giving voice at the side of the stage.)*

GIRL

Kokhava?

> *(Noor and Kokab look to the side as if someone has entered, then look down as if at a little girl.)*

KOKAB

Hello, Haya. What's wrong? I thought you were asleep.

HAYA

Do you need any help, Auntie?

KOKAB

No thank you, dear one. You go back to sleep, okay?

NOOR

Shalom.

                    HAYA

Shalom.

                    KOKAB

It's okay. This is the Rabbi's grandson.

                    HAYA

What is his name?

                    KOKAB

His –

                    NOOR

My name is Noor.

                    KOKAB

Looks like he knows some Hebrew.

                    NOOR

Where is she from?

                    KOKAB

Haya is from Hamburg in Germany.

                    NOOR

Hamburg! I know that name. Is it a big city?

                    KOKAB

Not after it was bombed.

                    NOOR

Did her family make it here?

        (Kokab sighs a little, doesn't answer.)

                    HAYA

What did he ask?

KOKAB

About your family. No. She's here by herself. The Germans took all the others.

NOOR

Oh.

KOKAB

During the bombing she made her way out until some of our people found her. Haya, love, you go to sleep now, okay?

HAYA

Okay.
Your name. What does it mean?

NOOR

Noor means "light". In Hebrew, you say "or".

HAYA

That's nice. Shalom, Or.

NOOR

Shalom, Haya.

HAYA

You are from the village of Kokhava?

NOOR

Yes.

HAYA

Kokhava does everything for us here.
Kokhava is our angel.
Good night, Kokhava.

KOKAB

Good night, dear one.

HAYA

Good night, Auntie.
Good night, Or.

NOOR

Good night, Haya.

*(They watch the invisible girl leave as the woman
giving voice to the invisible girl steps offstage.)*

NOOR

What will she do without family?

KOKAB

That's what we have to figure out.

NOOR

She could come live with us. In our village.

KOKAB

Mm. Just her?

NOOR

Well she doesn't have anyone else.

KOKAB

That's generous of you, Noor, but there are others without family.
Hundreds just in Tiberias. Can they all come live with you? You
think you have room for all of them in our little village? And all
of you?

NOOR

Yeah. There's room. We'll make room.

KOKAB

Go to sleep now. Things aren't always so easy, I'm afraid.

ZAKARIYA
(as he enters, standing at one side)

What was her name?

KOKAB

Hello Papa.

NOOR

Whose name?

ZAKARIYA

The little girl. I was listening. I didn't want to interrupt. What was her name?

NOOR

Haya.

ZAKARIYA

Haya.

NOOR

From Hamburg. In Germany.

ZAKARIYA

From Germany. So many of them.

(sits, wearily)

I was talking to some of the others as well. You're busy day and night.

KOKAB

And the next day and the next night.

ZAKARIYA

How do you do it?

KOKAB

Somebody has to.

ZAKARIYA

You're just like your mother. A caretaker without rest.

KOKAB

I'm glad she didn't live to see this.

ZAKARIYA

I suppose.

KOKAB

It might have changed her.

ZAKARIYA

It might have. It's worse than I understood.

(Pause.)

NOOR

Did you find Jamil?

ZAKARIYA

I found the captain. He doesn't know where Jamil is.

NOOR

He doesn't?

ZAKARIYA

Or if he does, he won't tell me.

(stands)

We have to go.

KOKAB

Right now?

ZAKARIYA

Yes.

KOKAB

It's late.

ZAKARIYA

Tofeek is waiting for us. We have a long walk and a long drive.

KOKAB

Papa.

ZAKARIYA

What.

KOKAB

Your place is here.

ZAKARIYA

Noor, let's go.

NOOR

Right now?

ZAKARIYA

(ushering him out impatiently)

Yes.

KOKAB

Papa. These people need you.
I need you.
It was too much for Mama and it's too much for me.

(They stop. Zakariya turns to her.)

ZAKARIYA

We're not spending the night here.

KOKAB

We're winning, Papa. Is that what you don't like? We're stronger now,
there are more of us, and we're winning. Is that why you're in a hurry?

ZAKARIYA

So winning and losing and winning, fighting forever, nothing but
fighting.

KOKAB

If that's what we're given, then yes. You still haven't understood.
Papa. Papa. There was no Red Sea that parted this time. There was

no Pillar of Fire. The Angel of Death did not Pass Over but chose
our people instead. The Angel of Death chose us. I don't know God's
plan, I don't even know if God has a plan but if God has a plan then
it's us. Just us. And we're strong. We are the manna in the desert.
We are the land and the milk and the honey. We don't ask permission
anymore. All we have is ourselves, and this little place. In all the
world just this little place. That we build. That is ours. That nobody
gives, that we make and we call our own. And preserve with our lives
if we have to.

(Pause.)

ZAKARIYA

My place.
Is in our village.
Your place too, my love.
I look forward to seeing you there.

> *(Zakariya is silent, then pulls Noor away and off.*
>
> *Kokab looks after them, then turns and goes off
> opposite. The chairs are taken away.*
>
> *Grandpa storms on opposite. He is on the windy
> mountainside road that leads out of the village to
> the east and north, where he has been waiting for
> Zakariya and Noor to return.)*

GRANDPA

God damn it, god damn it, god damn it, god damn it. Now what do we do?

(Enter Tofeek, Zakariya and Noor.)

TOFEEK

What's the hurry anyway?

GRANDPA

Anh, the Mukhtar got an itch and decided we should all leave right
away. Nothing about Jamil?

ZAKARIYA

No. They didn't know or they didn't tell me.

GRANDPA

Gooood damn it. I was just with Jamil's dad promising him you were on your way with Jamil. Now what do we do? We can't leave Jamil's dad here. Fattin will have to stay with him, then your mother won't go, then her mother won't go . . .

TOFEEK

We shouldn't go, any of us.

GRANDPA

Everybody's already gone. Our family is the last because we were waiting for you. Rabbi, I hope it's okay, Fattin went to your house and packed a few things for you.

ZAKARIYA

That's fine, I guess. Where will everyone go?

GRANDPA

We have cousins in Lebanon. Some people have family, others can stay with us, we'll figure it out. It's only for a few days, let these soldiers come and see we don't mean any trouble. Come on, let's get to your house and get your stuff.

(digs in pocket, pulls out a couple of old-fashioned keys on rings, hands one to Noor)

Noor, go back to the house and check if you need anything else.

NOOR
(taking key, but holds it out again)
Okay. These are Abu Kamal's.

GRANDPA
(takes the ring back, hands the other to Noor)
Anh, right, he gave me his too. Here. And not too much stuff! It's a couple days, not the Haj. Tofeek, let's go.

TOFEEK

You go ahead. I've got my truck.

GRANDPA

What?

TOFEEK

I won't run away.

GRANDPA

We're not running away. We're keeping safe while this blows over.

ZAKARIYA

He's right. You of all people should not stay here.

TOFEEK

Why me of all people?

ZAKARIYA

Because what are you gonna do, pull out your rusty old —

TOFEEK

Enough about the pistol! The Arab Legion will be here any day.

GRANDPA

Arab Legion? They're not even in this war yet.

TOFEEK

We can't just leave the whole village empty, with no one to watch it.

ZAKARIYA

Yes you can.

GRANDPA

We'll be back in a couple days.

TOFEEK

Someone should stay.

ZAKARIYA

Alright alright. Listen. I'll stay.

GRANDPA

What?

ZAKARIYA

I'll stay and guard everything. You go ahead.

GRANDPA

Why is everybody losing their minds?

ZAKARIYA

I'll be fine. I'll sit in the synagogue and pray till they're gone.

GRANDPA

I guess you think your holy books and the little yarmulke on your head are gonna protect you?

ZAKARIYA

They won't hurt me.

GRANDPA

We don't know what they'll do. You're coming with us.

ZAKARIYA

Who are you ordering around, old timer? I said I'm staying and I'm staying.

GRANDPA

God damn it. God damn it. What if I come back and you're not here?

ZAKARIYA

That could happen any time, to either of us. Sooner or later one of us will wake up and the other one gone. Don't worry. I'll be here. This is my village. It's easier for me to stay so I'm staying. Tofeek, if I stay, will you take your family and go with everyone else?

TOFEEK

Don't tell me what to do, Rabbi.

GRANDPA

Tofeek. Please. Listen for a minute.
I can't tell you what to do either. All I can say is this. Will you have mercy on an old man?

TOFEEK

What.

GRANDPA

Listen please. Losing you would be like losing another son. Do you hear me? Huh?

TOFEEK

I hear you.

GRANDPA

Alright. So shut the fuck up and go get your stuff. This crazy man will watch over the village for us.

TOFEEK

Well . . .

NOOR

I'm not leaving him here alone.

GRANDPA

Oh, terrific, now you're made him crazy too.

NOOR

If you're staying, I'm staying.

ZAKARIYA

Noor, listen. Listen. I'll be safe but you will not be. Do you hear me? You have to go and you have to go right now.

                            NOOR

Not without you.

                            GRANDPA

Crazy people are contagious. Noor, I know this old guy and he is
more stubborn than any donkey. Now he's decided, he'll stay now no
matter what, just so he doesn't have to admit he's nuts. But he's right
about one thing: he'll be more safe than you, and you will make it
more dangerous for him.

                            ZAKARIYA

It's true, Noor. You'll make it dangerous for me. I'll be fine and I'll
look after things.

                            TOFEEK

I don't want him snooping around my house.

                            NOOR

Why not?

                            TOFEEK

I don't trust him.

                            NOOR

Well I do trust him. Grandpa, wouldn't it be better if someone here
had the key to our house, in case anything happens? Here, Rabbi.

        (Noor looks at Tofeek, pointedly holds out the housekey
        to Zakariya.)

                            TOFEEK

What are you doing?

                            NOOR

It's time to know who our friends are. The Rabbi could have stayed
in Tabariya and been safe, but he chose to come back with us. Rabbi,
will you take these keys and take care of our house while we're gone?

ZAKARIYA

I'm pretty old, you know. Can't even carry a full bucket of water very far.

NOOR

You might not need to do anything. Just if anything goes wrong.

ZAKARIYA

Are you sure about this?

NOOR

You're someone we can trust. Isn't that right, Grandpa?

GRANDPA

Yes. Good idea. You're close by, you can look after things.

NOOR

Just in case.

GRANDPA

Just in case.

(holds out another key ring)
Here's Abu Kamal's keys also, next door.

NOOR

Yes. Why not? This is your village too, isn't it?

ZAKARIYA

(considers; then takes the keys)
It is. Alright. Not sure you need this, but alright.

GRANDPA

There now. *(sharply, for Tofeek's benefit)* If we can't trust you, who can we trust?

NOOR

That's right.

GRANDPA

This doesn't mean you should do anything stupid.

ZAKARIYA

God will protect the righteous. And maybe also me.

GRANDPA

It will take more than lamb's blood this time. But we'll be back real soon. You hear me? Nothing stupid. You keep yourself safe.

ZAKARIYA

I'll keep the backgammon board ready.

(They take hands for a moment. Grandpa and Tofeek turn and go but Noor hangs back a moment.)

NOOR

You're sure you're gonna be fine?

ZAKARIYA

Don't worry about me. You keep yourself safe and far away.

NOOR

Okay. This will pass over soon and we'll be back. Right?

ZAKARIYA

That's right. That's what we're hoping together.

(They look at each other for a moment. Noor shyly and uncertainly extends his hand – it's not usual for a young man to initiate with an elder. After a slight beat, Zakariya takes Noor's hand and they shake. They let go, look at each other, maybe nod a little, turn to leave in opposite directions. Noor goes off but before Zakariya leaves, Tofeek enters and goes to him to speak, privately and grudgingly.)

TOFEEK

If you're gonna be here anyway, my red peppers haven't seen water for two days.

(Tofeek leaves, Zakariya leaves opposite.

Lights and setting change.

Noor and Zakariya sit facing forward at opposite ends of the stage, side by side but far apart. Noor's arms are behind him, indicating that his hands are bound. Zakariya is not bound, but we might wonder if he is also a prisoner.

They sit in silence for a time. Neither looks at the other at first. Then Zakariya turns to Noor and asks:)

ZAKARIYA

Did they take anyone else?

(Noor shakes head. Silence.)

ZAKARIYA

How did they catch you?

NOOR

(calm, neutral, still does not look at him)
They didn't catch me. I came over the roofs.

ZAKARIYA

What happened?

NOOR

There was a soldier was in front of your house. I walked up to him and said I want to see the Rabbi.

ZAKARIYA

Why did you do that?

(Silence. Noor still does not look at him.)

NOOR

Did they torture you?

ZAKARIYA

No.

NOOR

Did they threaten you?

ZAKARIYA

No. They won't hurt me.

NOOR

I was up at the cave. I saw the soldiers come, and then the buses and
then Kokab with all those people. They're all from Tabariya, huh?

ZAKARIYA

You shouldn't have come back. Or you should have stayed in the cave.

NOOR

That cave isn't safe anymore.
If it ever had special power, it's gone.
I waited till dark to come down. I climbed up the old mulberry tree
and I could see you inside. I was gonna come in anyway but then I
saw something else.

ZAKARIYA

What?

NOOR

I could see through the window of my house. There were people
inside. They were sitting at the table. Using our plates.
I was able to get around to the front. I tried the door. The door was
locked.
I think they must have used a key. So I needed to come in and ask
you.

(finally turns to look at Zakariya.)

Did they use a key?

(Pause.)
(Pause.)

ZAKARIYA

Yes.

NOOR
(forcing himself to stay calm)
How did they get it? They didn't torture or threaten you. How did they get the key?

ZAKARIYA
I gave it to them.

NOOR
Why did you do that?

ZAKARIYA
So the soldiers wouldn't break down your door or knock down your whole house.

NOOR
You were saving our house.

ZAKARIYA
Yes.

NOOR
For who?

(Pause.)

NOOR
They're living in our houses. Until when?

ZAKARIYA
I don't know.

NOOR
What does that mean, you don't know? What did they say to you? Why are you letting them live in our homes?

ZAKARIYA
I'm not letting them do anything. It's not my decision.

NOOR

Did you go around handing out our keys yourself?

ZAKARIYA

They just would have smashed their way in. If you were here, they would have killed some of you and put others on trucks and driven you across the border. Without even the suitcases you took. At least you had those.

NOOR

I told my family they could trust you. I told everyone they could trust you.

ZAKARIYA

I saved your life just now.

NOOR

What saved my life? You made me a liar.

ZAKARIYA

You were on the list.

NOOR

What list?

ZAKARIYA

Your father was in the Arab Revolt. He was executed, and you might want revenge someday. Your uncle Tofeek was on the list too. They would have executed him if he had stayed.

NOOR

How did they get all our names?

ZAKARIYA

Yitzhak. Remember Yitzhak?

NOOR

Yitzhak and his rifles?

ZAKARIYA

Yitzhak was working for them all along. Mapping our village and our fields. Telling them names and faces. They've been preparing this for years, with people like Yitzhak all over Palestine. This wasn't a fight, it was a plan. You never had a chance of stopping them. And now when you were away and safe, you come back anyway. But because I am still a rabbi and still one of them, and because I gave them those keys, I was able to intervene. This one time. You were one reason they came here, but now you will stay alive.

(Pause.)

NOOR

You think I want you to keep me alive? They should kill me. You should go tell them to kill me. HEY! COME KILL ME –

ZAKARIYA

Noor stop it —

(Noor stands up, hands still held as if bound behind
him, starts toward the door; but Zakariya stands
in front of him, struggles with him both to restrain
and embrace. Noor shoves him away and steps back,
choking with what he is about to say.)

NOOR

You knew this was going to happen. In Tabariya. When we went to find Jamil.

ZAKARIYA

I knew they were coming. I begged the commander to pass us by. I told him this was a peaceful place. No reason to come here. He refused. He was ordered to clear the area of hostiles.

NOOR

Us.

ZAKARIYA

Yes. I hoped if they came I could change their minds.

NOOR

You knew and you didn't tell us what you knew.

ZAKARIYA

No, I didn't.

NOOR

Why not?

ZAKARIYA

Because I thought I could stop them. I still believed I could change
their minds. I was almost going to come with you, but I couldn't stop
believing that I could stand in front of them and they would agree
there was no reason to come into an empty village.

NOOR

But they came in anyway.

ZAKARIYA

Yes.

NOOR

And they stayed.

ZAKARIYA

Yes. I was wrong about many things. But then they told me what
their plan really is.

NOOR

What?

ZAKARIYA

To take everything. And call it their own. The orders came down
from their highest leadership. There was never any plan but taking it
all. All of Palestine. You couldn't have stopped them. The British are
letting them do it, and they're using all those weapons they got from
Europe. If any of you had stayed here, you would have been driven
out or worse. If you try to come back, they'll prevent you.

You won't be able to stop them. Nothing will stop them.

> ### NOOR

But you're gonna stay.

> ### ZAKARIYA

Yes.

> ### NOOR

Why?

> ### ZAKARIYA

My place is here. It's always been here

> ### NOOR

My place is here too. This is my place too.

> ### ZAKARIYA

I'm sorry. This is not what I wanted.

> ### NOOR

You gave them our keys.

> ### ZAKARIYA

To stop them from knocking your house down.

> ### NOOR

Is that why? To protect my house?
Is that why you gave them our keys?
Tell the truth now, Rabbi.
Is that why?

> *(Pause.)*

> ### ZAKARIYA

No.
Noor.
I stayed behind here and prayed for a miracle. For an actual miracle
that would save everybody and bring you back safe. I prayed hard.
But it didn't happen. What came was a different miracle. The buses

came up, and those people from Tabariya got off. I looked in their faces. They were squinting in the sunlight, they didn't know where they were. They were looking around for some kind of life. Some kind of help, some welcome.

And there was my daughter. Helping them find their way, tending to them. And I was so proud of her. And that's when I knew. These people are my task.

I'm not just the caretaker of some ancient synagogue floor anymore. There's a congregation here. Noor, I despise the fighting and the destruction, but maybe this is how it had to be. Maybe something good can be built here after all.

I'm glad to see you, I'm always glad to see you, but you should not have come back.

NOOR

And your congregation is going to live here. Like nothing happened. How are they going to do that?

ZAKARIYA

They don't know who was here.

NOOR

What do they think, there were just empty houses?

ZAKARIYA

They don't know what to think.

NOOR

Didn't they leave houses behind? With plates on the table and pictures still on the wall? Now they're walking into houses with plates on the table and pictures on the wall and they don't know what happened to make them empty? They're going to live here knowing what happened? What do you tell them, we faded away, we vanished? And you're gonna let them in your temple and show them your books and your cave and give them your holy blessing? You're going to live here with them knowing what happened?

(Pause.)

ZAKARIYA

They're my people now.

(Silence.)

NOOR

I am sorry you ever lived in our village.

ZAKARIYA

You don't mean that.

NOOR

I wish I did. I wish I did mean it.
I wish I had died without knowing you.
All those others out there. They're just conquerors like everyone
before them. They'll come and they'll go. They didn't do what you did.

(Noor sits, looking away from Zakariya. Silence.)

ZAKARIYA

I will find out what their plans are for you.

NOOR

You just told me what their plans are. They'll put me on a truck and
dump me across the border.

(Silence.)

ZAKARIYA

You should not try to come back. I won't be able to protect you if you
try to come back.

(Silence.)

ZAKARIYA

Greet your grandfather for me.

NOOR

He won't want to hear from you.

ZAKARIYA

Noor. Bad things happen in the world. Sometimes even a war will happen. We have to . . .

NOOR

No, Rabbi. You taught me something. War doesn't happen. People do it. People bring it. You had your choice and you chose to become one of them.

Go get your soldiers.

Go get your miracle.

And make me disappear.

(Silence.

Zakariya rises, walks across the room. Noor does not watch him go. After a long cross, Zakariya leaves without looking back.

Noor rises. Stands looking out past us, as he stood at the beginning.

NOOR

Did they ever tell you what they did with me?

They didn't take me to the border. Not right away.

First your soldiers took me to one of their prison labor camps at Sarafand. Then later they dumped me across into Jordan, with everybody else.

After nine years I found my family in Lebanon. Grandpa was dead by then. He never heard the truth from me, so he died without ever believing what you did.

(Noor looks out past us, seeing or hearing something distant.)

NOOR

Car coming.

I think your daughter called the police.

She really wants to forget.

(Pause.)

NOOR

I tried to stay away, Rabbi. But I couldn't.
I had to come see what died instead of me.

(Pause.)

NOOR

But that's not what I found.
I found our mulberry tree. Still alive
and still leaning over that wall between our houses.
My house is still there. Where I was born. Where I grew up.
And next door, Abu Kamal's house, where I grew up too.
And that's my synagogue. And over there
is my village's spring, still running.
When your soldiers came, you said
that nothing could stop them. You were wrong.
We don't vanish.
We don't fade.
We don't forget.
You should hope I remember how it was, Rabbi.
You should hope my children remember, and their children too.
Otherwise all our children will remember
is the last thing. What you did to us.
You really should hope we remember, Rabbi:
that this is how we lived.
And this is how we will live again.

(Lights down.)

the end

About the Authors

Hanna Eady and Edward Mast have been writing plays together since they met in Seattle in 1995. Hanna Eady grew up as a Palestinian in Northern Israel and had come to Seattle years earlier for graduate school in directing. Edward Mast was returning home from his first of many trips to the Occupied Palestinian Territories. Their first collaboration was *Sahmatah*, a play drawn from testimonies by residents of one of the Palestinian villages destroyed during the founding of Israel in 1948. *Sahmatah* premiered in 1996 in Seattle, and then premiered in Arabic in 1998 on the original site of the village itself inside what is now Israel. Other plays they have written together include *Loved Ones: Families of the Incarcerated*, *Letters from Palestine in the Time of the Virus*, and *The Love Tunnel: A Comedy of Occupation.*

Fomite

Writing a review on social media sites for readers will help the progress of independent publishing. To submit a review, go to the book page on any of the sites and follow the links for reviews. Books from independent presses rely on reader-to-reader communications.

More plays from Fomite...
Stephen Goldberg — *Screwed and Other Plays*
Michele Markarian — *Unborn Children of America*
William Damkoehler — *Self Storage and The Occupant*
David Schein — *Tokens: A Play on the Plague*

For more information or to order any of our books, visit:
http://www.fomitepress.com/our-books.html

Made in the USA
Monee, IL
08 October 2023

44195044R00121